3. 95

Volume Three

MY SERVANTS
THE PROPHETS

by

Dr. John T. Willis

BIBLICAL RESEARCH PRESS
774 East North 15th Street
Abilene, Texas
79601

MY SERVANTS

THE PROPHETS

Volume Three

By Dr. John T. Willis

Library of Congress Catalog Card No. 76-180789

PREFACE

There is no way for man to fully comprehend God's purposes and God's ways. Each new generation experiences the workings of God in history, sometimes manifesting Him in one way, and sometimes in another, but always in a way *relevant* to the problems and needs of each generation. As they sensitively recognize indications of God's work among them, all reflecting, believing men must exclaim with Paul:

> "O the depth of the riches and wisdom and knowledge of God! How unsearchable are his judgments and how inscrutable his ways!
> 'For who has known the mind of the Lord,
> Or who has been his counselor?'
> Or who has given a gift to him
> That he might be repaid?'
> For from him and through him and to him are all things. To him be glory for ever. Amen." (*Romans* 11:33-36).

The first two volumes in this series have dealt with the teachings of the eighth century prophets. In this volume, attention is focused on the work of Jeremiah, Zephaniah, Nahum, and Habakkuk, prophets who lived and preached in Judah about a hundred years after the days of Jonah, Amos, Hosea, Isaiah and Micah. The specific historical characters involved are different, but the religious principles involved are essentially the same.

The purpose of the following lessons is to emphasize the major teachings of the prophet Jeremiah (giving some attention to his contemporaries who were genuine prophets), to attempt to place them in proper perspective for modern day living, and to inspire the reader to desire the kind of life which they demand. May the God of Jeremiah dominate the lives of all who receive indications of his character by reading and studying this powerful prophetic book!

The Author

TABLE OF CONTENTS

LESSON

Lesson I

THE TURBULENT AGE OF JEREMIAH

"The Lord sent . . . bands of the Chaldeans, and bands of the Syrians, and bands of the Moabites, and bands of the Ammonites . . . against Judah to destroy it" (II Kings 24:2).

The Transition in World Power from Assyria to Babylon

In order to understand Jeremiah's message, it is necessary to have a basic knowledge of the major historical events which took place just before and during his prophetic career. Hezekiah of Judah (the last king during whose reign Isaiah preached) was succeeded by his son Manasseh, who had the longest reign of any Judean king (687-642 B.C.), and who was apparently the most wicked king that Judah ever had. During his reign, the Assyrian kings Esarhaddon (681-669 B.C.) and his son Ashurbanipal (669-633 B.C.) were quite successful in holding their vast empire together, in spite of attempts at rebellion in different locales at different times. But this proved to be very costly to Assyria, because her military exploits meant the loss of the lives of many soldiers and a growing weariness with constant fighting. Thus, shortly after Ashurbanipal's death, the great Assyrian empire began to crumble. The Scythians and Cimmerians made numerous invasions into the Assyrian domain from the North between 630 and 624 B.C. Nabopolassar became king of Babylon (626-605 B.C.) and successfully liberated Babylon from Assyrian domination. To the east, the Medes began to rise in power, and under their king, Cyaxares, they combined forces with the Babylonians in an attempt to throw off Assyrian rule once and for all. In a series of four major battles, the Assyrians were conquered, and Babylon became the new mistress of the ancient Near Eastern world. By examining a good map, it is easy to see that these battles took place at cities beginning in the east and moving to the west. This is the direction in which Assyria was forced to retreat before her conquerors. The first battle was fought at Ashhur in 614 B.C. Here the combined forces of Babylon and Media defeated the Assyrians. The second battle took place at the Assyrian capital of Nineveh in 612 B.C., and the forces of the Babylonians, Medians, and Scythians routed Assyria once again. Nahum had announced the doom of Nineveh about two years before this (see Lesson XIII). The third battle occurred at Haran, where the Scythians overran the Assyrians, as Zephaniah had announced (see Lesson XIII). When he learned that Assyria had been defeated at Haran, Pharaoh-Neco of Egypt led his army northward along the Mediterranean coastline to join forces with the Assyrians against the Babylonians at Carchemish. Foolishly, Josiah the king of Judah led the tiny Judean army in an encounter with Neco at Megiddo in Palestine, and was killed here at the height of his career (*II Kings* 23:29-30; *II Chronicles* 35:20-24). Four years later (in 605 B.C.), the son of Nabopolassar, Nebuchadrezzar II, led the Babylonian army against the combined forces of Egypt and Assyria at Carchemish. Assyria and Egypt were soundly defeated (Jeremiah 46). Not long after this battle, Nabopolassar died, and Nebuchadrezzar II made Babylon the new dominant power of the ancient Near East. Over the next several years, the Babylonians invaded Jerusalem three times, and the city fell in 587 B.C.

Circumstances in Judah

CHART I indicates the relationship of the last five kings of Judah, who ruled from 640 to 587 B.C.

CHART I

THE KINGS OF JUDAH DURING JEREMIAH'S CAREER

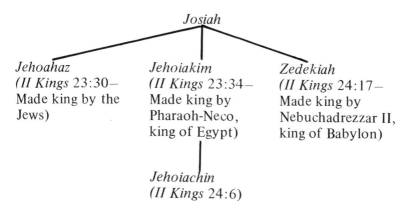

Josiah

Jehoahaz
(II Kings 23:30–
Made king by the
Jews)

Jehoiakim
(II Kings 23:34–
Made king by
Pharaoh-Neco,
king of Egypt)

Zedekiah
(II Kings 24:17–
Made king by
Nebuchadrezzar II,
king of Babylon)

Jehoiachin
(II Kings 24:6)

This Chart shows that three of these kings (Jehoahaz, Jehoiakim, and Zedekiah) were sons of Josiah, and one of them (Jehoiachin) was the grandson of Josiah, and the son of Jehoiakim. Let us examine the major events which occurred during the reigns of these kings pertaining to Jeremiah's career.

1. *Josiah* (640-609 B.C.). When Josiah came to the throne as a boy of eight (*II Kings* 22:1), the religious conditions in Judah were very bad because of the wicked reign of Manasseh and his son Amon. Manasseh had brought all sorts of pagan religious practices into Jerusalem. He rebuilt the high places which Hezekiah had torn down, erected altars for Baal, made an Asherah, worshipped the sun, moon, and stars (*II Kings* 21:3-5,7), burned his son in the fire as a sacrifice to Molech (*II Kings* 21:6; cf. *Jeremiah* 7:31-32; 19:4-6), practiced soothsaying, augury, and the like (*II Kings* 21:6), and promoted cult prostitution (*II Kings* 23:7).

At the age of twenty-six, Josiah was convicted that he must do something to restore the genuine worship of the Lord in Judah. He set about to repair the temple which had been profaned and broken through in many places over the past two generations. While this work was being done, the high priest Hilkiah found a copy of God's law somewhere in the temple area (*II Kings* 22:8). After this law had been pronounced authentic by the prophetess Huldah (*II Kings* 22:14-20), Josiah declared that the Jews must perform all that was written in it. A widespread reform was begun in 621 B.C. All elements of the worship of foreign gods were removed from the Jerusalem temple and Judah and burned (*II Kings* 23:4,6, 12-15), the idolatrous priests of these gods were deposed (*II Kings* 23:5), the prostitues were run out of the temple (*II Kings* 23:7), the high places in Judah were defiled and broken down (*II Kings* 23:8), the place where Manasseh and others had burned their sons in the fire to Molech in the Valley of the Son of Hinnom (Topheth) was defiled (*II Kings* 23:10), all types of sorcery were banned from the land (*II Kings* 23:24), and the Passover was reinstated as an annual religious practice (*II Kings* 23:21-23). Jeremiah, who had received his prophetic call five years earlier (626 B.C.—cf. *Jeremiah* 1:1-2), enthusiastically supported Josiah's reform at first (see *Jeremiah* 3:6-11), but when he saw that it was accomplishing little more than changes in the external forms of religion, he began to call the people to a genuine and complete change of heart and life (see *Jeremiah* 4:3-4).

At the peak of his career, Josiah foolishly engaged Neco of Egypt in battle at Megiddo when he was on his way to try to help Assyria against the Babylonians at Carchemish (see page 2), and the Egyptians killed Josiah.

2. *Jehoahaz* (609 B.C.). At Josiah's death, the Jewish people made Jehoahaz (or Shallum, see *Jeremiah* 22:10-12) his son their king. But this choice did not please Neco, so he took Jehoahaz into exile to Egypt and selected Jehoiakim (another son of Josiah) as the Judean king (*II Kings* 23:34). Thus the reign of Jehoahaz lasted only three months (*II Kings* 23:31).

3. *Jehoiakim* (609-598 B.C.). Jehoiakim was the vassal of Neco and Egypt from 609 to 605 B.C., when Nebuchadrezzar II and Babylon overran Assyria and Egypt at Carchemish.

After the battle of Carchemish, a portion of the Babylonian army came to Jerusalem and took some of its finest youths to Babylon to train them in Babylonian politics and customs. These included Daniel, Shadrach, Meshach, and Abednego (See *Daniel* 1). This was the first stage of the Babylonian captivity. From this time on, Jehoiakim was the vassal of Babylon. He did all he could to pacify first Neco, then Nebuchadrezzar, in order to satisfy his selfish desires. Jeremiah condemned him for his self-centeredness (*Jeremiah* 22:13-19). Because he denounced a mere external worship at the temple in the early part of Jehoiakim's reign (*Jeremiah* 7 and 26—see Lesson VII), Jeremiah was banned from going to the temple. Thus he dictated his oracles of doom to his disciple Baruch in the year 605 B.C. (*Jeremiah* 36:1-8). Baruch read them in the temple in 604 B.C. (*Jeremiah* 36:9), then to the princes, and finally to king Jehoiakim (*Jeremiah* 36:11ff). Jehoiakim became so angry that he cut up Jeremiah's scroll with a penknife and burned it in the fire (*Jeremiah* 36:23ff). Later, Jeremiah dictated his oracles to Baruch again, and added many similar words (*Jeremiah* 36:27-32).

4. *Jehoiachin* (598 B.C.). When Jehoiakim died, his son Jehoiachin became king. But he ruled only three months, because Nebuchadrezzar II sent the Babylonian army to besiege Jerusalem. They carried into captivity Jehoiachin and ten thousand of Jerusalem's leading citizens (*II Kings* 24:10-16) including the priest Ezekiel, who later received his prophetic call in Babylon in the fifth year of Jehoiachin's captivity (see *Ezekiel* 1:1-3). This was the second stage of the Babylonian captivity.

5. *Zedekiah* (598-587 B.C.). The last king of Judah was another son of Josiah named Zedekiah. After he had ruled as a vassal of Nebuchadrezzar II for nine years, he rebelled against his overlord, thinking that Pharaoh-Hophra of Egypt would deliver him from Babylon if worst came to worst (see *Jeremiah* 44:30). Babylon besieged Jerusalem for approximately a year and a half. During this whole period, Jeremiah urged Zedekiah to surrender to Babylon, but the Judean king would not listen. The siege was lifted when Nebuchadrezzar had to withdraw the Babylonian army from Jerusalem to fight Hophra, but (as Jeremiah predicted) this was only

temporary (*Jeremiah* 37:11-21), and Jerusalem and its temple were razed to the ground and burned in 587 B.C. and the Jews were carried into Babylonian exile. This was the third and final stage of the Babylonian captivity.

The End of Jeremiah's Career

After the fall of Jerusalem, the small number of Jews who were left in Judah were placed under a governor appointed by Babylon whose name was Gedaliah (*II Kings* 25:22ff). It seems likely that he ruled about five years (see the Commentaries on *Jeremiah* 40:7-41:18). At the end of this time, he was killed by a group of anti-Babylonian Jews led by a certain Ishmael. Then another group of Jews, whose leader was a man named Johanan, fled to Egypt for fear what the Babylonians might do to the Jews for killing the governor that they had appointed, and they forced Jeremiah and Baruch (against Jeremiah's will) to go with them (*Jeremiah* 43:5-7). In Egypt, Jeremiah continued to preach to God's people (*Jeremiah* 44). His prophetic career may have lasted until 580 or 575 B.C. Chart II provides a chronological table which will aid in a study of the life of Jeremiah, as well as that of his contemporaries Zephaniah, Nahum, and Habakkuk. It is hoped that the reader will refer to this Chart often as he studies the following lessons.

CHART II

A CHRONOLOGICAL TABLE PERTAINING TO JEREMIAH'S CAREER

Babylon	*Egypt*	*Judah*	*Judean Prophets*
Nabopolassar (626-605)	Ashurbanipal 669-633)	Josiah (640-609)	Jeremiah receives his call (626)
Conquest of Ashhur (614)		Josiah's reform (621)	Zephaniah (628-622
Conquest of Nineveh (612)			Nahum (614)

Conquest of Haran (609)	Pharaoh-Neco (609-593)	Josiah killed at Megiddo by Neco (609)	
		Jehoahaz (Shallum) (609)	
Conquest of Carchemish (605)		Jehoiakim (609-598)	
Nebuchadrezzar II (605-562)		Daniel and Jerusalem youths carried into Babylonian exile (605)—First Stage.	Habakkuk (605)
		Jehoiachin (Jeconiah, Coniah) (598)—Jehoiachin and 10,000 leading citizens carried into Babylonian exile—Second stage.	
			Ezekiel receives his call (593)
		Zedekiah (598 or 597-587)	
	Pharaoh-hophra (588-569)	Jerusalem razed to the ground and the temple burned. Many Jews carried into Babylonian captivity (587). Third stage.	
		Gedaliah governor over Judah (587-582)	Jeremiah and Baruch taken into Egypt (582)

REVIEW QUESTIONS

1. List in chronological order the four battles in which the Babylonians and/or their allies defeated the Assyrians, thus making Babylon the greatest world power in the ancient Near East. Give the date of each battle. Locate these places on a good map of the ancient world.

2. What were the circumstances surrounding Josiah's death? Discuss in detail.

3. Name at least five sinful practices that the wicked king Manasseh brought into Jerusalem during his long reign

4. What reforms did King Josiah carry out after Hilkiah discovered the copy of the law in the temple area?

5. In what way did Jeremiah support Josiah's reform? Why did he think this reform was inadequate?

6. Who was the king of Judah that was carried into Egyptian captivity?

7. Briefly enumerate and date each of the three stages of the Babylonian captivity. Check your answer by studying Chart II.

8. Who was the king of Judah who cut up and burned the scroll containing Jeremiah's oracles?

9. Who was the prophet that was carried into captivity when Jehoiachin and the ten thousand leading citizens of Jerusalem were carried away? When and where did he receive his prophetic call?

10. Who was the king of Egypt on whom Zedekiah depended against Babylon? Who was the Babylonian king whom burned down Jerusalem and the temple?

11. A few years after the fall of Jerusalem, where were Jeremiah and Baruch carried? Did this end Jeremiah's prophetic ministry?

Lesson II

GOD CALLS A YOUNG MAN
TO PREACH

"I appointed you a prophet to the nations" (Jeremiah 1:5).

God's Call

The scriptures teach that God places every man on earth at a specific time in human history in order to use him for His great purposes. No life is untouched by the divine hand, even if man fails or refuses to respond to his God-given opportunities. In the thirteenth year of the reign of Josiah of Judah (626 B.C.), God called a young man from Anathoth (about two miles north of Jerusalem) who was training to be a priest, to preach his message to the nations (*Jeremiah* 1:1-2). His name was Jeremiah. This was the culminating act of God in this man's life to this point, as is seen in the fact that God tells him that prior to the call He had known (or chosen) him, had formed him in his mother's womb, and had consecrated him (*Jeremiah* 1:5). Quite possibly, Jeremiah did not realize that God was working in his life until this call. So often, men are completely oblivious to divine influences on their lives until a challenging event takes place and forces them to reflect on their place in God's world.

Jeremiah's Reluctance

Unlike many men, Jeremiah possessed the rare ability to see himself as he really was. He was young (apparently about twenty years of age) and inexperienced, and he knew it. From attitudes indicated later in the book of Jeremiah, it seems likely that older leaders of the established religion in

Anathoth made sure that everyone knew that they were the ones who were in power, and no one, especially any youth in the land, was to "rock the boat." Jeremiah had not developed the art of public speaking. He recognized that by the standards of his day he was unable to "move an audience." Jeremiah was a "small town boy" from the tiny, unpretentious village of Anathoth. He had never travelled or "seen the world." What a shock it must have been when God appeared to him and announced, "I have appointed you a prophet *to the nations*" (*Jeremiah* 1:5). It is probable that the religious environment in which Jeremiah was raised had had a great influence on this thinking. Like Jonah, the prevalent view among Jewish leaders and people alike was that God had chosen Israel alone to be His people, and thus had no real concern for the nations. So, when God told Jeremiah he wanted him to preach to the nations, this cut directly across that which he had been taught to believe. With all these matters weighing on his mind, Jeremiah tried to reject the grave responsibility which God was attempting to get him to accept. He said, "Ah, Lord God! Behold, I do not know how to speak, for I am only a youth" (*Jeremiah* 1:6). In saying this, Jeremiah was not trying to put on a show of pious humility, but really believed that with his human limitations (the limitations placed upon him by his background and inherited traditional beliefs) he was not qualified to carry out God's important requests. It is this attitude of genuine self-subordination which is and always has been the key to successful service to God. Moses (*Exodus* 3:11), David (*Psalm* 51:10-13), Isaiah (6:5), and Paul (*I Corinthians* 15:9; *Ephesians* 3:8; *I Timothy* 1:15) are exalted in the Bible because they possessed this attitude.

God's Assurance

God refused to accept Jeremiah's excuses, sincere though they were. Rather, he insisted that this young man boldly do what God should tell him. He explained to Jeremiah that He was not asking him to carry the burdens that would surely come, once this work had begun. The success of such a mission did not ultimately depend on Jeremiah's age or speaking ability or background, but on God's power. As in every generation, the most vehement opponents whom Jeremiah could expect to encounter would be the political leaders of the established society and the religious leaders of the established church. But God assured the young man Jeremiah that He would not allow these tradition-bound opportunists to prevail against the preaching of God's word. He declares: "And I, behold, I make you this day a fortified city, an iron pillar, and bronze walls, against the whole land, against the *kings of Judah,* its *princes,* its *priests,* and the *people* of the land. They will fight against you; but they shall not prevail against you, for *I am with you,* says the Lord, to deliver you" (*Jeremiah* 1:18-19; see also verse 8).

The attitude and message which God thus gave Jeremiah differed radically from those to the average Jews of his day in two principal ways. First, God expected Jeremiah's feeling toward others to be positive instead of negative, to be inclusive instead of exclusive. While most of "God's people" around him took pride in the fact that *they alone* were the elect of God, Jeremiah was to have a genuine desire to bless and to save" the nations." When Jesus confronted the same sort of exclusivism in the Jews of his day, he said: "If you love those who love you, what reward have you? Do not even the tax collectors do the same? And if you salute only your brethren, what more are you doing than others? Do not even the Gentiles do the same?" (*Matthew* 5:46-47). It is easy for religious people in every generation to fall into this same narrow-minded exclusivism. Secondly, God commissioned Jeremiah to have an ultimate goal of *saving* the lost, not of rejoicing over their punishment, which must come because of their sin. To be sure, sin must be condemned. God told Jeremiah that he had set him "over nations and over kingdoms, to pluck up and to break down, to destroy and to overthrow." But He did not stop here. God's ultimate purpose in punishing individuals or nations is to bring them to their senses so that they will repent and turn to God for salvation. So God goes on to say that He had set Jeremiah "over nations and over kingdoms . . . to build and to plant" (*Jeremiah* 1:10). Criticism to achieve self-exaltation or criticism for criticism's sake has never been God's way with men. Like Jeremiah, every preacher, teacher, and Christian must strive to avoid misrepresenting God by wrong attitudes toward people.

The Vision of the Almond Rod

The account of Jeremiah's call is accompanied by two visions which emphasize two of the leading ideas which the prophet was to stress in his preaching. The Bible does not make it clear whether these were heaven-sent visions which the prophet saw with his physical eye, or pictures which appeared in his "mind's eye," or natural phenomena which had a special significance to him in explaining his message to others. The latter seems most likely.

The significance of the vision of the almond rod is based on a word-play or pun which appears in Hebrew. The word for "almond" is *shaqed*, and the word for "watching" is *shoqed*. Occasionally, this vision is interpreted to mean that God "awakes" early to carry out his word just as an almond tree is the earliest to "awake" (bloom) after winter. Not only does this explanation fail to appreciate the word-play in the Hebrew, but it also reads into the text the idea of an almond *tree*. The *rod* often occurs in scripture to denote punishment. The writer of Proverbs says:

> "Do not withhold discipline from a child; If you beat him with a *rod* he will not die" (*Proverbs* 23:13).

Isaiah 10:5,15 refers to Assyria as the *rod* of God's anger. So, in *Jeremiah* 1:11-12, the almond *rod* is a symbol of punishment. God commissioned Jeremiah to announce that sinful Judah and other nations would be punished (*Jeremiah* 1:10), and now he assures his prophet that He will carry out this punishment which he announces. This explains the word-play. Jeremiah sees a "rod of almond" (*shaqed*), and God explains that this means, "I am watching (*shoqed*) over my word (i.e., word of judgment) to perform it." This interpretation is supported by the use of this same word "watch" (*shoqed*) in *Jeremiah* 5:6; 31:28; 44:27.

The Vision of the Boiling Pot

Jeremiah sees a boiling pot "facing away from the north" (*Jeremiah* 1:13). The pot is tilted over toward the south so that its contents flow from north to south. God explains that this is symbolic of foreign nations sweeping down on Judah from the north and punishing her because she has forsaken God and burned incense to other gods (*Jeremiah* 1:14-16). In the immediate context of Jeremiah's historical situation, undoubtedly the reference is to the idolatry which Manasseh had brought into Judah. If this vision belongs to the same period as Jeremiah's call, it was given five years before Josiah began his reform and attempted to drive idolatry out of the land. A comparison with God's announcement of doom on Judah in *Jeremiah* 15:4 is instructive here: "I will make them (i.e., God's people) a horror to all the kingdoms of the earth because of what Manasseh the son of Hezekiah, king of Judah, did in Jerusalem." (See also II Kings 21:10-14; 23:12,26-27; 24:1-4). As the following lesson will show, "The Foe from the North" is a central theme in Jeremiah's preaching.

REVIEW QUESTIONS

1. Do you believe that God acts in the lives of people today to motivate them to serve him effectively? Discuss this in light of Jeremiah's call.

2. What three factors caused Jeremiah to reject God's commission when he first heard it?

3. Discuss the attitudes which the church should have toward young men growing up in its midst. Are there attitudes in the church which hinder a young man from serving God to his fullest potential?

4. Who were Jeremiah's severest opponents? Can you analyze why this was the case? Do you find similar situations existing in the twentieth century church?

5. In what two ways did Jeremiah's attitude and message differ from those of God's people in his day?

6. What is the meaning of the vision of the almond rod?

7. What is the meaning of the vision of the boiling pot?

Lesson III

NO WAY TO ESCAPE

"Be sure your sin will find you out" (Numbers 32:23).

Under the wicked influences which had been brought into Jewish life during the reign of Manasseh, sin had grown and taken deep root in the hearts of all facets of society, from the religious and political leaders to the poor and downtrodden. Of course, God's intention was that his people be happy and prosperous. But as they sinned more and more, His love for them demanded that he do everything possible to keep them from destroying themselves. Since they did not respond to gentler methods, he was forced to resort to punishment. Human punishment is often vengeful, but God's punishment is a genuine indication of the depth of His love for mankind. The writer of Proverbs says (3:11-12):

> "My son, do not despise the Lord's discipline
> Or be weary of his reproof,
> For the Lord reproves him whom he loves,
> As a father the son in whom he delights"

Israel was determined to continue in sin; thus, God had to punish them—they brought it on themselves. When punishment comes, Jeremiah declares:

> "Have you not brought this upon yourself
> By forsaking the Lord your God?" (*Jeremiah* 2:17).

And again he says:

> "Your ways and your doings
> Have brought this upon you" (*Jeremiah* 4:18).

The purpose of this lesson is to call attention to some of the ways in which Jeremiah tried to warn God's people that doom lay in their future if they did not repent and turn to the Lord, and to convince them that this doom was no accident of history, but rather was a manifestation of God's positive concern for His people.

The Foe from the North

The meaning of the Vision of the Boiling Pot in *Jeremiah* 1:13-16 is that God is going to send invading armies into Judah from the North in order to punish them for their idolatry and apostasy. Many of the doom-oracles in the book of Jeremiah repeat this theme. For example, God declares:

> "Raise a standard toward Zion,
> Flee for safety, stay not,
> For I bring evil *from the north*,
> And great destruction" (4:6).

In another place he announces:

> "Behold, a people is coming *from the north country*,
> A great nation is stirring from the farthest parts of
> the earth" (6:22).

(See also 6:1; 10:22; 13:20). It is clear from *Jeremiah* 25:9 (which is dated in 605 B.C., i.e., the fourth year of Jehoiakim, see v. 1) that in later years of his ministry, "the foe from the north" was the Babylonians. But it is possible that in some of his earlier oracles, possibly dating from the reign of Josiah (like 4:6, perhaps), that Jeremiah had the Scythians in mind. Be this as it may, when Jeremiah speaks of the foe from the north, he emphasizes that God was working among the nations of the world to carry out His purposes. It is *God* who says, "*I* will send for all the tribes of the north" (25:9), or "*I* bring evil from the north" (4:6). The biblical speakers and writers assume that God is a God who continually works in the lives of individuals and nations to accomplish His purposes.

A Seventy Year Captivity

In 605 B.C. (see *Jeremiah* 25:1), Jeremiah announced

that because of the multitude of Judah's sins, God would carry His people into Babylonian captivity, where they would stay for seventy years. He said: "This whole land shall become a ruin and a waste, and these nations shall serve the king of Babylon seventy years" (25:11). (See also 25:12; 29:10). Most people in Judah assumed that since they were *God's* people, dwelling in *God's* land, and worshipping at *God's* house (the temple), surely God would not allow anything so severe to happen to them. Not long after Jehoiachin and 10,000 citizens were carried away into Babylon in 598 B.C. (see Lesson I), the prophet Hananiah challenged the genuineness of Jeremiah's message, and announced "in God's name" that God would return Jehoiachin and all the Jewish exiles in Babylon to Judah "within two years" (28:3-4). But Jeremiah held his ground. He knew that Judah's sin was too great for such a brief punishment like two years of captivity. In the same year (see 29:1), he wrote a letter to the exiles in Babylon, and told them to "settle down" in their new environment, because they would be there for seventy years (29:10), as he had said before. If God had not carried his punishment through to its end, it would not have taught his people the seriousness of sin in the way that He had intended.

It is interesting to note that in 536 B.C. (70 years after 605 B.C.), some of the Jews in Babylonian captivity returned to Jerusalem under the leadership of Zerubbabel and Joshua to rebuild the temple, as Cyrus, King of Persia, had authorized (cf. Ezra 1).

Terror on every side

Jeremiah lived in an age when nations and God's people alike operated under the shadow of false security. The nations felt secure because of their military might and human wisdom, and the Jews felt they were secure because they not only had military might and human wisdom, but they also had been chosen by God to receive special blessings. Thus, on several occasions, Jeremiah announced that "terror was on every side," and thus there was no way for sinners to escape the punishing wrath of God. Once, after Jeremiah had announced that Jerusalem and its temple would be destroyed by the Babylonians, the chief officer of the temple, a man named Pashhur, put Jeremiah in stocks (20:1). When he released him the next day, Jeremiah gave him the symbolic name of "Magor-missabib," which is a Hebrew expression meaning *"Terror is on every side"* (20:3). Then he explains: "For thus says the Lord: Behold, I will make you a terror to yourself and to all your friends. They shall fall by the sword of their enemies while you look on. And I will give all Judah into the hand of the king of Babylon . . . And you, Pashhur, and all who dwell in your house, shall go into captivity" (20:4,6).

In 605 B.C., when Pharaoh-neco and Assyria joined forces against Nebuchadrezzar and Babylon at Carchemish, Jeremiah delivered an oracle concerning Egypt, announcing their defeat. In this oracle he says:

> "They are dismayed
> And have turned backward.
> Their warriors are beaten down,
> And have fled in haste;
> They look not back—
> *Terror on every side* (Hebrew—*Magor-missabib*)"
> (46:5).

Again, when Nebuchadrezzar advanced against Kedar and the kingdoms of Hazor, Jeremiah issued an oracle, in which he said: "Men shall cry to them: *'Terror on every side!'* " (49:29). But also, in one of his oracles announcing the coming of the "foe from the north" into Judah to punish them for their sins, Jeremiah declares to the people:

> "Go not forth into the field,
> Nor walk on the road;
> For the enemy has a sword,
> *Terror is on every side*" (6:25).

Apparently, the reason Jeremiah emphasized this theme: "Terror on every side," is that he wanted to make it clear to the sinners whom he addressed that there was no way for them to escape the consequences of their actions. Similarly, Paul compares sin with a seed which produces fruit after its own kind, when he writes: "Whatever a man sows, that he will also reap. For he who sows to his own flesh will from the flesh reap corruption" (*Galatians* 6:7-8).

God's Concern

Jeremiah uses three human relationships to explain why God punished His people when they sinned. (a) God loved Judah as a husband loves his wife. During Josiah's reign (possibly in connection with Josiah's reform), Jeremiah delivered an oracle in which he compared (North) Israel's response to God's love with (South) Judah's response. He pointed out how Israel had left her husband (the Lord) and went after other lovers (the Baals), and how God divorced Israel because of her unfaithfulness, sending her into exile (Jeremiah 3:6-8). But he says that Judah did not learn anything from her sister's fate. "Her false sister Judah did not fear, but she too went and played the harlot" (3:8). God was personally involved in Judah's life because she was his wife. (b) God loved Judah as a father loves his child. Thus, even when He had to punish him, He was doing what was best for him. He says:

> "Is Ephraim my dear son?
> Is he my darling child?
> For as often as I speak against him,
> I do remember him still.
> Therefore my heart yearns for him;
> I will surely have mercy on him" (31:20).

(c) God cared for Judah's well-being like a physician cares for the well-being of his patient. As a physician, God analyzes the depths of Judah's sin:

> "Your hurt is incurable,
> And your wound is grievous.
> There is none to uphold your cause,
> No medicine for your wound,
> No healing for you" (30:12-13; see also 8:22).

But in spite of this, God offers divine healing, which can overcome all diseases, including sin. He cries:

> "I will restore health to you,
> And your wounds I will heal" (30:17).

Such love, which reaches out to the most rebellious and sinful of men, defies human comprehension.

REVIEW QUESTIONS

1. What is there about God's love which causes Him to punish sinners?

2. Why do sinners have to suffer?

3. According to Jeremiah, how was God going to punish Judah historically for their sins?

4. Give two possible identifications of the "Foe from the North." Do you believe that God is working in the affairs of nations today? Discuss.

5. How long did Jeremiah predict that the Jews would be in Babylonian captivity? When did this period begin? In what event was it fulfilled?

6. Concerning what four people or groups of people did Jeremiah announce "terror on every side?" What is the Hebrew expression for this? What is the religious significance of this expression?

7. What are three human relationships that Jeremiah used to emphasize the reason why God was concerned about His people, so that when they sinned he punished them?

Lesson IV

SIN - AN ESTABLISHED HABIT

"The more I called them,
The more they went from me;
They kept sacrificing to the Baals,
And burning incense to idols" (Hosea 11:2)

Man tends to be a creature of habit. In every aspect of life (daily routines, social patterns, ways of dealing with personal and group problems, etc.), he reacts to pressures and attempts to carry out his aspirations by repeating techniques which seem to work for himself and others in a practical way. At the same time, man has the capacity to struggle with life's perplexities creatively. On the one hand, sin entices man to establish habits which will ultimately destroy him; on the other hand, God is willing to give man the inner strength to struggle against his temptations and rise above them, so that ultimately he can enjoy the rich blessings of life and be saved.

During Jeremiah's lifetime, God's people yielded more and more to the temptations of idolatry, pride, self-centeredness, trust in human power, etc., which the world around them offered. Sin became their way of life. It was not because individual Jews committed sins now and then as they sincerely struggled to overcome their temptations that Jeremiah announced their impending doom, but because they had sold out to sin—the people were no longer struggling against sin. As Jeremiah puts it:

'The prophets prophesy falsely,
And the priests rule at their discretion;
My people love to have it so" (5:31).

Judah's Sin is Long-lived and Deep-rooted

The way in which Jeremiah tried to deal with this problem was to illustrate to God's people in various ways that they had made sin a way of life. His examples are striking, and merit careful attention:

(1) The Jews thought of their service to God as drudgery. They felt like they were in prison with God as the jailor. Sin looked enjoyable, so they "burst their bonds", shook their fist in God's face (as it were), and said, "I will not serve" you any longer (2:20). Every individual must cope with the problem of *why* he serves God. Is it out of a sense of duty, or is it a matter of gratefully responding to God's love? (see *Matthew* 11:28-30; *I John* 5:3). One's answer to these questions determines the quality of his relationship to God.

(2) God's people yielded themselves to all kinds of idols just as a harlot submits herself to any man who will pay her price (2:20). "Because harlotry was so light to her, she polluted the land, committing adultery with stone and tree" (3:9). God shows his disgust with the way His wife was behaving, when he says:

> "Where have you not been lain with?
> By the waysides you have sat awaiting lovers
> Like an Arab in the wilderness" (3:2).

How inconsistent it is for God's people to become so vehemently opposed to physical harlotry, only to regularly practice spiritual harlotry!

(3) Like a husbandman, God had planted Judah in the promised land as a choice vine of pure seed, but she had gradually declined to a degenerate wild vine by repeated sinning (2:21).

(4) Judah's sin had become such an integral part of her life that one could not speak of God's people without thinking of sin. "God's people" and "sin" had become equated. It was like a man who spent all his time working in filth and dirt. Any time he would make an effort to get clean,

even the strongest detergents could not remove the grime, since it had become a part of his body. So God says to Judah:

> "Though you wash yourself with lye and use much soap,
> The stain of your guilt is still before me" (2:22).

(5) Sinners have a way of repeating the same group of destructive patterns. Using an illustration which was immediately comprehensible to ancient man, Jeremiah compares God's people with "a restive young camel interlacing her tracks" (2:23). In modern terms, we might say "they had gotten into a rut," or "they were going around in circles," or "they are spinning their wheels."

(6) Although her life was filled with sin, Judah displayed a great show of religion. In this way, she believed she was "pulling off" the "perfect crime." Her main concern was to get what she wanted any way she could "without getting caught." God compares His people with a thief:

> "As a thief is shamed when caught,
> So the house of Israel shall be shamed;
> They, their kings, their princes,
> Their priests, and their prophets,
> Who say to a tree, 'You are my father,'
> And to a stone, 'You gave me birth.'
> For they have turned their back to me,
> And not their face.
> But in the time of their trouble they say,
> 'Arise and save us!' " (2:26-27).

(7) The Jews had become so steeped in sin that it was impossible for them to overcome temptations in and of their own power. It would have been as difficult for Judah to get rid of her sins as it would be for an Ethiopian to change the color of his skin and still be an Ethiopian, or for a leopard to get rid of his spots and still be a leopard. Jeremiah asks:

> "Can the Ethiopian change his skin
> Or the leopard his spots?
> Then also you can do good
> Who are accustomed to do evil" (13:23).

(8) When ancient man wanted to preserve something for posterity, he inscribed it deeply into a rock with a writing chisel (see Job 19:23-24). Thus, in order to describe the extent of Judah's sin, Jeremiah declares: "The sin of Judah is written with a pen of iron; with a point of diamond it is engraved on the tablet of their hearts" (17:1). One thing, then, could be said about God's people in Jeremiah's day—they were well-trained in the art of sin. It was a vital part of their way of life.

> "They are skilled in doing evil,
> But how to do good they know not" (4:22).

Self-Centered Motivations

The major reason that God's people were so steeped in sin is that they were determined to get what they wanted at any cost. Their primary motivation for every act they did was not what God willed or what would best benefit others, but what would be in their own best interest.

a. They strove to build a strong army and powerful military defences, and they trusted in this might. But God announced that He was sending a nation against Judah to divest them of this object of trust.

> "Behold, I am bringing upon you
> A nation from afar, O house of Israel . . .
> Your fortified cities *in which you trust*
> They shall destroy with the sword" (5:15,17).

b. The rich increased in wealth at the expense of the poor, and felt secure in this wealth. But Jeremiah says:

> "Like the partridge that gathers a brood which she
> did not hatch,
> So is he who gets riches but not by right;
> *In the midst of his days they will leave him,*
> And at his end he will be a fool" (17:11).

c. Man's mind is a wonderful gift from God. But it is possible for men to take credit for their own knowledge and trust in their own mental capacities instead of in God. Thus, Jeremiah encountered those who boasted of their wisdom.

On one occasion he said: "Thus says the Lord: 'Let not the wise man glory in his wisdom, let not the mighty man glory in his might, let the rich man glory in his riches; but let him who glories glory in this, that he understands and knows me, that I am the Lord who practices steadfast love, justice, and righteousness in the earth; for in these things I delight, says the Lord" (9:23-24). On another occasion he declared:

> "Cursed is the man who trusts in man
> And makes flesh his arm,
> Whose heart turns away from the Lord.
> He is like a shrub in the desert,
> And shall not see any good come.
> He shall dwell in the parched places of the wilderness,
> In an uninhabited salt land" (17:5-6).

The Linen Waistcloth

One way in which the prophets taught was to perform symbolic acts in the sight of the people to arouse their curiosity, and then show them the spiritual application of what they were doing (see Volume I, Lesson VI). At God's direction, on one occasion Jeremiah bought a linen waistcloth, carried it to the banks of the Euphrates River, and hid it in a cleft of a rock. Later, he returned to recover the waistcloth and found that it was spoiled and good for nothing (13:1-7). Then God explained to Jeremiah what this symbolized—"Thus says the Lord: Even so will I spoil the *pride* of Judah and the *great pride* of Jerusalem. This evil people, who refuse to hear my words, *who stubbornly follow their own heart* and have gone after other gods to serve them and worship them, shall be like this waistcloth, which is good for nothing" (13:9-10).

Jeremiah announced that Judah and Jerusalem would be punished (see Lesson III). But this punishment originated from God, and was necessitated by the fact that Judah had sold out to sin, and that little or no struggle against sin existed any longer among them as God's people.

REVIEW QUESTIONS

1. Analyze yourself! Enumerate some of your habits! Do you feel these are good habits or bad ones? Do you feel that you could change these habits? Could you do this alone? Could you do it with God's help?

2. List the eight illustrations suggested in this lesson which Jeremiah used to try to convince the people of Judah that they had made sin a way of life.

3. Do you enjoy serving God, or is it a drudgery? Be as honest as possible in answering this and discussing it. Do you know people who apparently are miserable in their service to God? Can you explain why you or they are miserable?

4. Do you feel you are growing spiritually, or that you are "spinning your wheels?" Try to analyze the reason for this. What can be done to improve this situation?

5. Are there things which you would really like to do, but you do not do them because you are afraid that you would get caught? Do you feel these things are wrong within themselves? Do you feel others need to change their attitudes toward these things, or that you need to re-examine your own heart to see if you desire to do something which is not good for you?

6. Name three things in which God's people trusted in the days of Jeremiah. Do you feel that God's people are faced with the same problems today? Discuss.

7. Discuss Jeremiah's lesson based on the linen waistcloth. Do you think this lesson is relevant today?

Lesson V

A FRANTIC SEARCH FOR A RIGHTEOUS MAN

"And I sought for a man among them who should build up the wall and stand in the breach before me for the land, that I should not destroy it; but I found none" (Ezekiel 22:30).

The Power of Vicarious Living

All Bible students are familiar with the striking story of Abraham's intercession for Sodom when God announced that He intended to destroy this wicked city. Abraham had a special interest in Sodom because his nephew, Lot, and his wife and two daughters were living there at the time. So he prayed fervently that God would spare the city for the sake of just a few righteous people, if they could be found; and God agreed. It was a tragedy that there were less than ten righteous people living in Sodom, and the city had to be destroyed.

Later, before God finally allowed the Babylonians to destroy Jerusalem and the temple, he sent Ezekiel through the streets of the chosen city in search for just one man whose life was of such sterling quality that he could justify God sparing the city, but he could not find one (*Ezekiel* 22:30). It seems incredible that God's own people allowed sin to control their lives so completely.

In a similar way, God told Jeremiah and his companions:

"Run to and fro through the streets of Jerusalem,
Look and take note!
Search her squares to see if you can find a man
One who does justice and seeks truth;
That I may pardon her" (5:1).

These three examples assume that the righteous, though they may be few in number, provide a quality to human society which allows it to continue to survive. A righteous man lives *vicariously* for his wicked neighbor. This is the point which Jesus made so often, as when he said to his handful of disciples, "You (plural) are the salt of the earth" (*Matthew* 5:13), or "You (plural) are the light of the world" (*Matthew* 5:14), or when he said, "The kingdom of heaven is like leaven which a woman took and hid in three measures of meal, till it was all leavened" (*Matthew* 13:33). Such a beautiful concept gives purpose to living a righteous life, because in so doing one is touching the lives of others, even if only indirectly, and is blessing them.

The Depth of God's Concern for Sinners

Why does God allow sinners to continue in sin day after day without punishing them or destroying them? Man cannot know the answer to this in every instance. But a careful study of *Jeremiah* 5 and 6 seems to indicate that basically it is because of God's very nature.

> "He is gracious and merciful,
> Slow to anger, and abounding in steadfast love,
> And repents of evil" (*Joel* 2:13; *Jonah* 4:2; *Exodus* 34:6; *Psalm* 103:8).

If He can bring man to repentance without using drastic means, God prefers to work in this way. He does not enjoy making men suffer. In obedience to God's charge, Jeremiah first went to the poor. To many people, poverty is synonymous with righteousness. However, although it is true that if a person is divested of all material securities, he *may* be more inclined to trust in God for help, this is by no means always the case. The Bible warns against the temptations of poverty as well as the temptations of wealth. One writer says:

> "Two things I ask of thee,
> Deny them not to me before I die:
> Remove far from me falsehood and lying;
> *Give me neither poverty nor riches;*
> Feed me with the food that is needful for me,

Lest I be full, and deny thee,
And say, 'Who is the Lord?'
Or lest I be poor, and steal,
And profane the name of my God" (Proverbs
30:7-9).

Jeremiah could not find a single poor man who was righteous. God looked for "truth," i.e., genuineness, in the poor, but he found only hypocrisy, so the prophet says:

"O Lord, . . . thou hast consumed them,
But they refused to take correction.
They have made their faces harder than rock;
They have refused to repent" (5:3).

Now, Jeremiah turns to the religious leaders ("the great") of God's people, for he reasons that "they know the way of the Lord, the law of their God," but he finds with deep remorse that:

"They all alike had broken the yoke, They had burst
the bonds" (5:5).

There is a great difference between knowing a thousand verses of scripture from memory and serving God with all the heart. Just because a person is a preacher or a Bible teacher or a bishop or some other sort of church leader does not mean that his heart is filled with and motivated by Godlike attitudes.

Undoubtedly, Judah was ripe for punishment. But God still longs to spare his people from suffering if at all possible. So, one last time he sends Jeremiah through the city in search of one righteous man. He says to his prophet:

"Glean thoroughly as a vine the remnant of Israel;
Like a grape-gatherer pass your hand again over its
branches" (6:9).

Yet, once again the search was in vain. Jeremiah says with great disappointment:

"The word of the Lord is to them an object of scorn,
They take no pleasure in it" (6:10).

And again, he cries:

> "For from the least to the greatest of them,
> Every one is greedy for unjust gain;
> And from prophet to priest,
> Every one deals falsely" (6:13).

It is only after God has exhausted every other means that He resorts to punishment as an avenue to reach the hearts of the lost.

The Art of Rejecting the Responsibility for Sin

When Jeremiah confronted God's people with their sins, they denied that they were guilty. The prophet quotes some of his hearers as saying, "I am innocent; surely his anger has turned from me," and "I have not sinned" (2:35). On another occasion, some of the people ask Jeremiah (apparently with sincere looks on their faces): "Why has the Lord pronounced all this great evil against us? What is our iniquity? What is the sin that we have committed against the Lord our God?" (16:10). Instead of accepting the responsibility for their own sins, the people of Jeremiah's day blamed previous generations for bad conditions which existed around them. A proverb circulated widely among the Jews:

> "The fathers have eaten sour grapes,
> And the children's teeth are set on edge" (31:29).

(See also *Ezekiel* 18:2). Jeremiah denied that God was punishing the present generation merely because the former generation had sinned. He said, "Every one shall die *for his own sin;* each man who eats sour grapes, his teeth shall be set on edge" (31:30). On another occasion, he declared, "You have done *worse than your fathers,* for behold, every one of you follows his stubborn evil will, refusing to listen to me" (16:12).

The Bible contains many illustrations of sinners who tried various ways to avoid accepting responsibility for what they had done. Adam blamed the woman and God (for giving him the woman) (*Genesis* 3:12), and the woman blamed the serpent (*Genesis* 3:13). Saul blamed the people (popular pressure) for sparing some of the sheep and oxen after defeating the Amalekites (*I Samuel* 15:20-21). Aaron attributed the golden calf which he had made to accident, when he said, "And I said to them (i.e., the people of Israel), 'Let any who have gold take it off'; so they gave it to me, and I threw it into the fire, *and there came out this calf" (Exodus* 32:24). Of course, many similar examples could be cited. There is something about sin which makes the guilty sinner want to keep it a secret. A certain shame comes in the same package as the momentary pleasure of committing a sinful act. This is a universal and timeless experience for all sinful mankind.

The Importance of Objects of Love

Man usually does what he loves. Judah loved self, and thus she served self. She was attracted by the pleasure-filled orgies which accompanied the worship of the Baals, so she forsook the Lord and went after these others gods. Then, the Lord asked Israel this question:

> "What wrong did your fathers find in me
> That they went far from me,
> And *went after worthlessness, and became worthless?"* (2:5).

Such a statement seems to indicate that a man is the product of all the things which he genuinely loves. This emphasizes the care which must be taken in selecting the objects of one's love in all aspects of life.

REVIEW QUESTIONS

1. Give three examples suggested in this lesson which teach that God wanted to spare a group of people, but could not do so because so few righteous people could be found among them. In what ways do you feel that righteous lives can be a blessing even in a wicked society? Discuss.

2. Has it ever entered your mind that God was not punishing sinners as quickly as they deserved? Discuss possible explanations for this.

3. In light of the scriptures given in this Lesson, and in light of your own personal study of the Bible, discuss the relationship between righteousness and poverty on the one hand, and between wickedness and wealth on the other.

4. To what two groups did Jeremiah go in search of a righteous man?

5. What is it that better qualifies a person to preach or teach or be an elder, etc.; to commit hundreds of verses of scripture to memory; or to understand the major emphases which the Bible intends to convey, and to strive to apply these principles to modern problems and situations? Is there any direct relationship between memorizing scripture and godlike attitudes and actions? Discuss.

6. Give some examples of people who tried to avoid accepting the responsibility for the sins they had committed. Do you think people today behave in a similar manner? Discuss.

7. As honestly as possible, list the five things which you love the most. Compare these things with those of others in the class and discuss the items which are more interesting to the class. Are you aware that these things are molding your attitudes and actions? Discuss.

Lesson VI

DEVELOPING RIGHT ATTITUDES TOWARD SINNERS

"Those who are well have no need of a physician, but those who are sick" (Matthew 9:12).

The Critical Eye of the Self-Righteous

It is well-known that the book of Jeremiah (and the Bible as a whole for that matter) is filled with oracles condemning the wicked. Those who feed on "constantly looking for things to criticize" in others use condemnations in the Bible as "proof texts" to justify their own self-righteousness. And yet, strangely, they do not realize that they themselves rest under the condemnations of God, since Christ condemned the attitude of the Pharisee who said: "God, I thank thee that I am not like other men" (*Luke* 18:11). It is difficult for such people to see that there is a great difference between Jesus' statement: "the *gate* is narrow . . . that leads to life" (*Matthew* 7:14), and their own theology, which seems to hold that "the *mind* is narrow that leads to life." Jesus is here speaking paradoxically (as He often does), and means that the *narrow gate* is accessible only to the truly *broad minded*. What a tragedy it is to confuse the *narrow gate* with the *narrow mind!*

Good men condemn sin by their words and by their lives. But they do not do so with the attitude of the self-righteous, who are basically arrogant. They do it with humility, always aware of the fact that they too are sinners and really stand under the same condemnation. They do not seek to hurt others, and thereby exalt themselves; but rather, their overwhelming desire is to save other sinners as a physician saves the life of his patient. This was the attitude which lay behind Jeremiah's preaching.

The Necessity of Sympathetic Understanding

The man who cannot put himself in the sinner's place, feel the depth of his temptations with him (psychologists call this empathizing), and offer him help out of a genuine concern for his well-being, is not the kind of man God needs for preaching, teaching, personal work, mission work, or anything of this sort. When God called Jeremiah, he manifested the quality most essential for a genuine man of God—he recognized how limited and inadequate he himself was.

Jeremiah had to announce the doom which was about to come on God's people through the invading Babylonians, and he had to trace the cause for this to the sins of Judah, but Jeremiah did not enjoy this work. He was not glad that his people were destroying themselves. He was one of them, and what he wanted more than anything else was for them to return to God and receive his blessings. Again and again, his marvellous attitude is reflected in the book. He says:

> "My grief is beyond healing,
> My heart is sick within me.
> Hark, the cry of the daughter of my people
> From the length and breadth of the land . . .
> For the wound of the daughter of my people is my heart wounded,
> I mourn, and dismay has taken hold on me.
> Is there no balm in Gilead?
> Is there no physician there?
> Why then has the health of the daughter of my people not been restored?
> O that my head were waters,
> And my eyes a fountain of tears,
> That I might weep day and night
> For the slain of the daughter of my people!"
> (8:18-19, 21-22; 9:1).

On another occasion, when he is pleading with God's people

to forsake their own interests and turn to God, Jeremiah declares:

> "But if you will not listen,
> My soul will weep in secret for your pride;
> My eyes will weep bitterly and run down with tears,
> Because the Lord's flock has been taken captive"
> (13:17).

In one of his dialogues with God, Jeremiah makes it clear that he did not enjoy telling the Jews that they were on a course headed for destruction. He says:

> "I have not pressed thee to send evil,
> Nor have I desired the day of disaster,
> Thou knowest" (17:16).

The Beauty of Interceding for Others

Jeremiah was the kind of sensitive soul who repeatedly asked God to give His people just one more chance or just a little longer to repent. For example, he says: "So let it be, O Lord, if I have not entreated thee *for their good,* if I have not *pleaded with thee on behalf of the enemy* in the time of trouble and in the time of distress!" (15:11). On another occasion he says:

> "Remember how I stood before thee *to speak good for them,*
> *To turn away thy wrath from them"* (18:20).

Some would accuse Jeremiah of being "soft" in taking such an attitude toward sinners. They would say that he was *permissive.* But the truth is that he was manifesting the same attitude as God did toward His people. This is the way a father feels toward his rebellious son. The Lord says on one occasion:

> "Is Ephraim my dear son?
> Is he my darling child?
> For as often as I speak against him,
> I do remember him still.
> Therefore my heart yearns for him;
> I will surely have mercy on him" (31:20).

Of course, a man like Jeremiah can persist in praying and interceding for God's people beyond that which God himself knows is best. And several times in the book of Jeremiah, we find the Lord telling Jeremiah not to intercede for the people any longer because they had persisted in sin (7:16; 11:14; 14:11). But man acts more in the spirit of God when he is lenient than when he is constantly critical.

Beginning with People where they are

Paul once reminded Christians at Ephesus of their behavior and attitudes before they accepted Christ. He said:

> "You were dead through the trespasses and sins in which you once walked, following the course of this world, following the prince of the power of the air, the spirit that is now at work in the sons of disobedience. Among these *we all* once lived in the passions of our flesh, following the desires of body and mind" (*Ephesians* 2:1-3).

As long as Christians can honestly remember and acknowledge their own sins, they can appreciate the problems which others are facing. But sometimes, God's people forget what they once were, and become very intolerant of their fellow men. Such an attitude destroys the useful purposes which God intends for His people to serve on earth in the capacity of blessing the lives of sinners.

Jeremiah's behavior toward God's sinful people can best be explained by the fact that he was not concerned about running people down and catching them in sin, but about gently helping them rise above their sins to serve God with all their heart. He began where they were. He constantly remembered how spiritually immature he was when God called him. He did not expect everyone to become like he was "in the twinkling of an eye." He realized that growth can occur only over a long period of time, and that neither he nor his hearers would ever become exactly what God wanted them to be.

No two people are exactly the same, even if they are

children raised in the same home. Each person undergoes a long series of events which no one else on earth ever experiences. Thus, it is quite possible that a person who "appears" to be *below* another person spiritually has actually made much more progress than the other, because he has had to overcome so many more sinful influences and problems in his life. It is little wonder, then, that Jesus warns: "Pass no judgment, and you will not be judged . . . Why do you look at the speck of sawdust in your brother's eye, with never a thought for the great plank in your own? Or how can you say to your brother, 'Let me take the speck out of your eye', when all the time there is that plank in your own? You hypocrite! First take the plank out of your own eye, and then you will see clearly to take the speck out of your brother's" (*Matthew* 7:1,3-4). Because God is not interested in "showing people up," but in saving them, He often acts much slower than men with critical eyes would have him work, but His purposes always vindicate the method under which he operates.

REVIEW QUESTIONS

1. What was Jeremiah's attitude when he condemned sinners and warned them that they were headed for destruction? Do all preachers, teachers, and Christians have this attitude when they voice their disapproval of sin? What is your own personal attitude? Discuss.

2. Do you believe that Jesus (or God) wants his people to be "narrow minded?" Discuss this in light of the way in which Jesus treated the adulterous woman who washed his feet (*Luke* 7:36-50).

3. Do you feel that a preacher can truly minister to the needs of people without putting himself in their place and sympathizing with them in their problems? Discuss this.

4. Discuss the attitude which Jeremiah manifests as recorded in *Jeremiah* 8:18-9:1; 13:17; and 17:16.

5. Do you feel that God and Jeremiah were "permissive" because they tried to be gentle and loving with the sinful people whom they were trying to save? How would you have dealt with these people?

6. Have you always lived the kind of life you are living now? What changes have you made in your attitudes and in your life habits? Do you find yourself criticizing people for things which you used to do? How should you think of and deal with these people?

Lesson VII

THE MASQUERADE OF REPENTANCE

"This people honors me with their lips,
But their heart is far from me" (Matthew 15:8).

Circumcision of the Flesh and Circumcision of the Heart

Judged on the basis of "visible responses," Jeremiah was certainly a "successful preacher", at least during the reign of Josiah. The book of Jeremiah has preserved several instances in which his preaching led to "confessions of sins" on the part of his hearers. The first of these is recorded in 3:22-4:4. Jeremiah makes a heart-stirring appeal for the people to repent. He announces God's invitation:

> "Return, O faithless sons,
> I will heal your faithlessness" (3:22a).

Immediately, the people respond with choice words.

> "Behold, we come to thee;
> For thou art the Lord our God...
> "From our youth the shameful thing has devoured all for which our fathers labored . . . For *we have sinned* against the Lord our God, . . . from our youth even to this day; and *we have not obeyed* the voice of the Lord our God" (3:22b,24,25).

How impressive these words sound! Who could doubt that the sinful people were touched by Jeremiah's preaching? But God looks on the heart (see *I Samuel* 16:7), and it is clear to Him that these people have no intention of changing their attitudes or their way of life, but are *using religion* in order to avoid punishment and assure divine protection. Thus, God calls for "truth", i.e., genuineness (4:2), and says:

> "Break up your fallow ground,
> And sow not among thorns.
> Circumcise yourselves to the Lord,
> Remove the foreskin of your hearts" (4:3-4).

Unless the heart is first prepared for God's word as a farmer prepares the ground for sowing seed, there is little prospect for spiritual growth. Unless the heart is truly "circumcised", fleshly circumcision (in which the Jews constantly took pride) is of little value. This same thought is emphasized in *Jeremiah* 9:26, "all the house of Israel is uncircumcised in heart," and in *Romans* 2:28-29, where Paul says:

> "For he is not a real Jew who is one outwardly, nor is true circumcision something external and physical. He is a Jew who is one inwardly, and real circumcision is a matter of the heart, spiritual and not literal."

Quantity and Quality

On another occasion, Jeremiah's hearers acknowledge their sins and plead for God's help. They say:

> "Though our iniquities testify against us,
> Act, O Lord, for thy name's sake;
> For our backslidings are many,
> *We have sinned* against thee . . .
> Why shouldst thou be like a stranger in the land,
> Like a wayfarer who turns aside to tarry for a night?
> Why shouldst thou be like a man confused,
> Like a mighty man who cannot save?
> Yet thou, O Lord, art in the midst of us,
> And we are called by thy name;
> Leave us not" (14:7-9).

As sincere as these words may seem at first, under careful analysis it becomes clear that these people were more concerned to receive the promise of God's blessings than they were to change their lives. Because of this, God refuses to accept them (14:10) and forbids Jeremiah to intercede in their behalf (14:11). He renounces their fasting and sacrifices, not because these are contrary to God's will, but because they are no substitute for a genuine change of heart and life. God declares: "Though they fast, I will not hear their cry, and though they offer burnt offering and cereal offering, I will not accept them" (14:12).

Flattery and Service

Sinners seem to have a peculiar knack for praising God and flattering the church. In this way, they (perhaps subconsciously) seek to make God and men feel ashamed to rebuke them for their hypocrisy and lack of commitment. Jeremiah encountered this sort of response from God's people in his day. They said in prayer to God:

> "Why hast thou smitten us
> So that there is no healing for us? . . .
> We acknowledge our wickedness, O Lord, . . .
> For *we have sinned* against thee . . .
> Are there any among the false gods of the nations
> that can bring rain?
> Or can the heavens give showers?
> Art thou not he, O Lord our God?
> We set our hope on thee,
> For thou doest all these things" (14:19,20,22).

These people must have thought that surely God would not reject the pleas of those who flattered him so eloquently and so highly. But people are transparent to God—He can see right through their facade and outward show. Thus, He replies to their cries: "Though Moses and Samuel stood before me, yet my heart would not turn toward this people. Send them out of my sight, and let them go!" (15:1). There is a great difference between "flowery words" or "verbal resolutions", and real day by day service to God.

Jeremiah's Sermon on the "Church Building"

In the beginning of the reign of Jehoiakim (about 598 or 597 B.C., perhaps), Jeremiah went to the Jerusalem temple, where the Jews came to worship God in great multitudes on the sabbath day and high feast days, and preached an important "sermon" on the temple (*Jeremiah* 26:1). This "sermon" is recorded in two places in the book of *Jeremiah,* viz., in chapters 7 and 26. Basically, it contains three points, each of which is of vital significance for a correct understanding of the nature of true religion.

(1) The popular belief that regular attendance at the temple (or any church building) guarantees God's continued care and protection, is false. Jeremiah cries out: "Do not trust in these deceptive words: 'This is the temple of the Lord, the temple of the Lord, the temple of the Lord.' " (7:4). It is common for "religious" people to judge "church growth" on the basis of Bible school attendance, church attendance, annual or weekly contribution, the number of hospital or home visitations made, and the like. Jeremiah denies that these are acceptable criteria. The real basis for determining church growth is the attitudes of church members toward God, one another, and the world.

(2) The sort of "religion" which God desires consists in helping the poor, the orphans, the widows, and all who are in distress as a sincere expression of compassion for suffering humanity. Jeremiah explains it this way: "If you truly amend your ways and your doings, if you truly execute justice one with another, if you do not oppress the alien, the fatherless or the widow, or shed innocent blood in this place, and if you do not go after other gods to your own hurt, then I will let you dwell in this place" (7:5-7). Some would ridicule such a concept of religion by labelling it a "social gospel," but the Bible (New Testament as well as Old) describes it as "pure (true, genuine) religion" (*James* 1:27; see *Luke* 10:25-37).

(3) It is possible to make the temple (or the church building) a hideout for crooks rather than a hospital for penitent sinners. Jeremiah asks: "Will you steal, murder, commit adultery, swear falsely, burn incense to Baal, and go after other gods that you have not known, and then come and stand before me in this house, which is called by my name, and say, 'We are delivered!'—only to go on doing all these abominations? Has this house, which is called by my name, become *a den of robbers* in your eyes?" (7:9-11). Every generation is faced with the problem of "religionists" who use their piety, their regularity in church attendance, as a smoke screen to cover up or hide their real motives and

their real deeds. To use the language of *I Timothy* 6:5, they "imagine that godliness is a means of gain."

Jeremiah's powerful "sermon" calls for a fresh re-evaluation of "religious" aspirations, motivations, and concepts. It is interesting that when Jeremiah first preached this sermon, the "religious" leaders and people of Judah almost sentenced him to death (see *Jeremiah* 26:11), and did ban him from going to the temple any more to worship (36:5). Undoubtedly, they accused him of "not loving the church," of being a "young rebel," and of "trying to stir up strife." It is ironical that "religious" people want the preacher to condemn everyone but themselves, and when the preacher must reprove them because of their ungodly attitudes or behavior, they are most violent. Let us be careful today about condemning some "unsound" preacher or teacher who may in fact sound very much like Jeremiah in his message.

REVIEW QUESTIONS

1. Are "visible responses" to "good preaching" a sure indication of "church growth?" Discuss.

2. What two illustrations did Jeremiah use to urge the people of God to turn to God with all their heart? Make some modern applications of this principle.

3. Can religion be used as a means to insure people against calamity? Discuss.

4. Is it possible that beautiful prayers and songs can be used as a means of flattering and bribing the church and God to avoid making the sinner face his life as it really is? Discuss.

5. What three lessons did Jeremiah teach in his "sermon" on the temple? Discuss each of these, and make applications to the modern day situation.

6. In your opinion, does religion involve helping the poor, providing for orphans and widows, and upholding the destitute, or is this merely a social gospel which true preachers should avoid?

7. How was Jeremiah treated when he preached his sermon on the temple? Do you know of instances in which the church today has treated preachers in a similar way?

LESSON VIII

THE AWESOME RESPONSIBILITY OF LEADING GOD'S PEOPLE

"From the prophets of Jerusalem
Ungodliness has gone forth into all the land" (Jeremiah
23:15).

The Quality of Leadership in Judah

It is not often that a people is able to rise above the teaching and example of its leaders. Therefore, it is most important that God's people in particular choose men who are eminently qualified to lead them. Those who do not know the contents of God's word, or who do not put the various elements of God's word in proper perspective, or who do not sincerely wish to help God's people improve, or those whose lives are not disciplined for good, or whose hearts lack love for others, eventually lead God's people astray.

The book of Jeremiah is filled with condemnations of four groups of leaders in Judah who had failed the people by poor teaching or bad example:

(1) Jeremiah often rebukes the king and his royal princes. For example, in the tenth year of Zedekiah (about 588 B.C.), God announces: "This city (i.e., Jerusalem) has aroused my anger and my wrath, from the day it was built to this day, so that I will remove it from my sight because of all the evil of the sons of Israel and the sons of Judah which they did to provoke me to anger—*their kings and their princes,* their priests and their prophets, the men of Judah and the inhabitants of Jerusalem" (32:31-32; see also 1:18;

2:26; 8:1; 24:8; 34:18-21; etc.). Good and just political leaders are important for the well-being of any people.

(2) Since he had been trained for the priesthood, Jeremiah was particularly sensitive to the sins of the priests of Judah. He says:

> "From prophet to *priest*,
> Every one deals falsely" (6:13; 8:10).

Again, he remarks:

> "Both prophet and *priest* ply their trade through the land,
> And have no knowledge" (14:18).

And on another occasion he says:

> "Both prophet and *priest* are ungodly;
> Even in my house I have found their wickedness"
> (23:11).
> (See also 1:18; 2:8, 26: 5:31; 13:13; 20:1; etc.).

(3) Many of the same verses pertaining to the priests also refer to the prophets. *Jeremiah* 23:9-40 is devoted almost exclusively to reproving the prophets for their false teachings and promises. God declares that the prophets are a burden which God must bear because they are leading the people astray (23:33).

(4) Jeremiah also condemns the wise men or wisdom teachers. In one oracle he says:

> "How can you say, 'We are wise,
> And the law of the Lord is with us'?
> But, behold, the false pen of the scribes
> Has made it into a lie.
> The *wise men* shall be put to shame,
> They shall be dismayed and taken;
> Lo, they have rejected the word of the Lord,
> And what wisdom is in them?" (8:8-9).
> (See also 9:12, 23; 18:18).

One gets the impression from reading the book of Jeremiah

that all levels of leadership in Judah during Jeremiah's day were corrupt.

The Message of Judah's Leaders

Judah's prophets, priests, wise men, and princes taught the people a traditional doctrine, which had its roots in God's choice of Israel in Egypt and his deliverance of his people at the Exodus. Thus, it was not difficult for them to make it sound "scriptural." Actually, the problem was not that they did not know the basic facts of Israel's religious heritage, but that they did not apply them correctly to their own contemporary situation. Their message may be summarized generally in this way.

(1) They affirmed that because the Jews were the people of God, God would not allow them to suffer destruction or to be driven out of the promised land of Canaan. So, Jeremiah says:

> "They have spoken falsely of the Lord,
> And have said, 'He will do nothing;
> No evil will come upon us,
> Nor shall we see sword of famine' " (5:12).

This is what Jeremiah has in mind when he condemns the prophets, saying:

> "They have healed the wound of my people lightly,
> Saying, 'Peace, peace,'
> When there is no peace" (6:14; 8:11).

What these prophets meant was that there was no reason for the people to be concerned about the danger of calamity, because God would not let anything so drastic happen to them. Jeremiah makes this clear when he says: "They say continually to those who despise the word of the Lord, 'It shall be well with you'; and to every one who stubbornly follows his own heart, they say, 'No evil shall come upon you.' " (23:17).

(2) Judah's leaders also taught the people that if they would perform the external acts of worship regularly, this

would guarantee their well-being. God rebuked the people for adopting such an inadequate view of religion, and charged them to change their attitudes and their way of life. For example, he asks: "What right has my beloved in my house, when she has done vile deeds? Can vows and sacrificial flesh avert your doom?" (11:15). Again He questions:

> "To what purpose does frankincense come to me
> from Sheba,
> Or sweet cane from a distant land?
> Your burnt offerings are not acceptable,
> Nor your sacrifices pleasing to me" (6:20).

God has always been vitally concerned with attitudes which motivate human actions. The book of Jeremiah is filled with admonitions to God's people to change their hearts. On one occasion, God declares:

> "The heart is deceitful above all things,
> And desperately corrupt;
> Who can understand it?
> I the Lord search the mind
> And try the heart,
> To give to every man according to his ways,
> According to the fruit of his doings" (17:9-10).
> (See also 4:4; 9:25-26; 29:13; 31:31-32).

While the Jewish leaders were telling God's people that God would not allow them to be defeated and to be carried into exile, Jeremiah kept on insisting that it was God's will that they be carried into exile, and that, therefore, they should surrender to Babylon. (a) On one occasion, he bought a potter's earthen flask, and then invited some of the elders and senior priests of the Jews to go with him into the valley of the son of Hinnom, south of Jerusalem. When they arrived, Jeremiah declared that the Lord was going to destroy Jerusalem because the sins of God's people were so great (19:1-9). Then he broke the flask in their sight as a symbolic act, and explained: "Thus says the Lord of hosts: So will I break this people and this city, as one breaks a potter's vessel, so that it can never be mended" (19:11). (b) During the siege of Jerusalem in 589-587 B.C. (see 21:2), Jeremiah delivered an oracle to the people on "the way of life and the way of death." He explained that "the way of death" (by which he meant, the sure way to die physically) is to stay in Jerusalem and fight against the Babylonians, and that "the way of life" (by which he meant, the sure way to stay alive physically) is to surrender to the Babylonians and let them carry the people into exile (21:8-10). (c) A few years before this, shortly after Jehoiachin (Jeconiah) and 10,000 of the leading citizens of Jerusalem had been carried into Babylonian exile (about 597 B.C.), Jeremiah related a vision which he had seen. He saw two baskets of figs before the Jerusalem temple. One basket contained good figs, and the other bad. He explained that the basket of good figs represented those who were carried into captivity, since they had a bright future, and that the basket of bad figs represented Zedekiah and the Jews who were left in Jerusalem, since they would be overthrown by the Babylonians (*Jeremiah* 24).

Because of his message, it is not surprising that politically Jeremiah was considered to be a traitor, a rebel, and unpatriotic, and that religiously he was rebuked and treated as a heretic and a false teacher. (Lesson IX deals with the opposition which Jeremiah encountered). It is interesting to speculate as to what Jeremiah would preach in the modern world and church, and as to how he would be received.

The Deeds of Judah's Leaders

Unfortunately, the piety of Judah's leaders did not extend far beyond the walls of the "church building." In their every day living, they were the "chiefest of sinners." To cite one concrete incident, king Jehoiakim built himself a beautiful home, but he did this by hiring poor people to do the work, and then refusing to pay them their rightful wages. Thus, Jeremiah rebukes him by saying:

> "Woe to him who builds his house by unrighteousness,
> And his upper rooms by injustice;
> Who makes his neighbor serve him for nothing,
> *And does not give him his wages;* . . .
> Do you think you are a king
> Because you compete in cedar?
> Did not your father eat and drink

And do justice and righteousness?
Then it was well with him.
He judged the cause of the poor and needy;
Then it was well.
Is not this to know me? says the Lord.
But you have eyes and heart
Only for your dishonest gain. . . " (22:13,15-17).

Jeremiah condemns the religious and political leaders of God's people for for all sorts of sins, such as adultery (5:8; 9:2); dishonest business dealings (5:26-27; 9:4-6); greed (6:13; 8:10); stealing, murder, false swearing (7:9), pride (9:23-24), and neglect of their fellow men, especially the widows, orphans, and poor (5:28).

Like the great eighth century prophets and the New Testament, Jeremiah emphasizes that the essence of service to God is to love God and one's fellow-man with all the heart (see *Matthew* 22:36-39), or to put it another way: "Religion that is pure and undefiled before God and the Father is this: to visit orphans and widows in their affliction, and to keep oneself unstained from the world" (*James* 1:27).

REVIEW QUESTIONS

1. Evaluate the *quality* of leadership in the church in general and in your own local congregation or community. List the strong points and the weak points. In your opinion, how can this situation be improved?

2. Name the four groups of leaders which Jeremiah condemned. Give one reason why he condemned each group. Do these faults exist in leaders in the church today?

3. What was basically wrong with the teaching of Judah's religious leaders? Does this sort of teaching exist today?

4. What two themes appear again and again in the teaching of Judah's leaders? Can these themes be detected in the modern church?

5. How did the emphasis in Jeremiah's teaching differ from that of the religious leaders of his day? Do you think this emphasis is still relevant today?

6. What three symbolic acts and visions did Jeremiah use to show that Judah was destined for destruction and exile?

7. What kind of lives did Judah's religious and political leaders display? Can the same sort of thing be found among religious leaders today?

Lesson IX

THE PERILS OF PREACHING AND TEACHING GOD'S WORD

"I was like a gentle lamb led to the slaughter" (Jeremiah 11:19).

Methods of Persecuting God's Messenger

The Bible is filled with cases of persecution against God's messengers. It is ironic that many of these persecutions originated with, and were carried out by, those who professed to be God's own people. Jesus was persecuted by the Jews, and Paul by men claiming to be Christians and even apostles. Jeremiah belongs to the same category. It is not difficult to understand that, like Jesus and Paul, he was persecuted because he dealt with the way the people thought and lived day in and day out, and he did so in a practical manner, which all his hearers could comprehend. Sermons using "big words" or ambiguous phrases, and couched in traditional terminology, make men popular preachers, but do not reach into the heart of individuals and of society to remove masks of hypocrisy and to bring men to repentance and salvation. In every generation, God's people have repeated the same established human methods of persecuting preachers and teachers who proclaim God's word with a Christlike attitude, instead of what they want to hear. These methods are reflected in the way in which the religious and political leaders of the Jews persecuted Jeremiah. They warrant careful consideration.

1. One way of persecuting a preacher is to refuse to take seriously and to put into action the word of God which he preaches. On one occasion, Jeremiah urged his hearers to

return to the teaching of the Law of Moses (the ancient paths) and the earlier prophets (watchmen), but they refused. He said:

> "Thus says the Lord:
> 'Stand by the road, and look,
> And ask for the ancient paths,
> Where the good way is; and walk in it,
> And find rest for your souls.'
> *But they said, 'We will not walk in it.'*
> 'I have set watchmen over you, saying,
> 'Give heed to the sound of the trumpet!'
> *But they said, 'We will not give heed.' "* (6:16-17).

2. Often, people ridicule the message and work of a preacher. Jeremiah laments:

> "I have become a laughingstock all the day;
> Every one mocks me" (20:7).

When Jeremiah appeared in public with a wooden yoke around his neck to symbolize the fact that Judah would be under the yoke of Babylon for seventy years, the prophet Hananiah walked up to Jeremiah, jerked the yoke-bars off his neck, and broke them, declaring that the Jews would not be in exile for more than two years (28:10-11).

3. Another method of ruining a preacher is to make accusations against him in order to cast reflection on his good name. When the siege was lifted from Jerusalem temporarily, Jeremiah set out to go to the land of Benjamin in order to receive his portion there among his people, but a sentry by the name of Irijah arrested him and accused him of deserting to the Babylonians (37:12-13). In spite of Jeremiah's protests to the contrary, he was cast into prison on the charge of being unpatriotic and a traitor to his country (37:14-15). After the governor, Gedaliah, was murdered, certain Jews came to Jeremiah and asked him if it was the Lord's will that they stay in Judah or flee to Egypt. Jeremiah said that they should stay in Judah. But several of these Jews accused him of telling a lie (43:1-2). *Jeremiah* 18:18 tells how the religious leaders of Judah plotted against Jeremiah, saying, "Come, let us smite him *with the tongue.*"

4. Some people become so violent that they try to harm God's spokesman physically. When Jeremiah announced that Jerusalem and its temple were going to be destroyed like a broken potter's vessel (chapter 19), the priest (the chief officer of the temple!), Pashhur, "beat Jeremiah the prophet, and put him in the stocks" (20:2).

5. Like Paul, Jeremiah was often cast into prison for what he preached (see 36:26; 37:15, 21; 38:28; 39:15). On one occasion, he was forbidden to preach any more in the temple because his words were so despised (36:5).

6. Jeremiah's life was often in jeopardy because he preached God's word. Some of the earliest threats on his life came from those who knew him best—the men of Anathoth (11:21), the men of his own home town (1:1). Even Jeremiah's own family sought to harm him because of what he preached. Thus, God says to Jeremiah:

> *"Even your brothers and the house of your father,*
> Even they have dealt treacherously with you;
> They are in full cry after you;
> Believe them not,
> Though they speak fair words to you" (12:6).

When Jeremiah preached his sermon on the temple (the church building), the religious leaders were vehement and said: "This man deserves the sentence of death, because he has prophesied against this city" (26:11; see also v. 8). Perhaps one of the best known stories concerning Jeremiah is the one in which he was cast into an old, abandoned cistern and left to die because he announced the downfall of Jerusalem (38:1-6).

Jeremiah's Reactions to Persecution

Jeremiah was a human being who was trying to bring sinful people back to God. He acted differently under different types of persecutions which were brought against him at different times. (a) Sometimes he simply tried a new way to reach the hearts of the people. For example, when he was banned from going to the temple (36:5), he dictated his words to one of his disciples named Baruch, and sent him to read his message to the people (36:4-8). (b) At other times, Jeremiah warned those who persecuted him of the inevitable consequences of their actions. For example, when the chief officer of the Jerusalem temple, Pashhur, beat Jeremiah and put him in the stocks, Jeremiah warned him that he and all his friends would be carried into Babylon and never return to Palestine (20:6). And when the prophet Hananiah jerked the yoke-bars off of Jeremiah's neck and said that the Babylonian captivity would last no more than two years, Jeremiah said to him: "Listen, Hananiah, the Lord has not sent you, and you have made this people trust in a lie. Therefore thus says the Lord: 'Behold, I will remove you from the face of the earth. This very year you shall die, because you have uttered rebellion against the Lord'" (28:15-16). The next verse states that this came to pass. (c) On other occasions Jeremiah prayed for his enemies and those who persecuted him (15:11; 18:20). About six hundred years later, Jesus instructed His disciples to deal with their enemies in the same way (Matthew 5:44-45). (d) Several times, Jeremiah became very angry, and asked God to destroy his enemies who were persecuting him (11:20; 15:15; 17:18; 18:21-23). Perhaps his bitterest prayer is found in 18:23:

> "Thou, O Lord, knowest all their plotting to slay me.
> Forgive not their iniquity,
> Nor blot out their sin from thy sight.
> Let them be overthrown before thee;
> Deal with them in the time of thine anger."

Such a prayer is hardly exemplary for God's people. And yet, it should be remembered that no man of God has ever felt right and acted right toward those who persecuted him *at all times and under all circumstances* (except Jesus). Like all preachers and teachers, Jeremiah was a human being and guilty of sin.

A Modern Application

This lesson has a much more practical application than many in the modern church are willing to admit. Each year, a number of sincere young men with good minds enter the

Christian ministry (remember that Jeremiah was a young man when he entered the ministry). They naturally assume that their primary task is to seek for and preach truth, and that the church will support them with encouragement, enthusiasm, and money as they do this. As these men grow intellectually and spiritually, they often come to realize that they cannot accept and preach some of the church traditions, and that they cannot adopt some of the attitudes of church members, because they sincerely believe that these conflict with the teachings of the Bible.

As preachers and teachers, like Jeremiah these men feel compelled by God to preach what is true and what is essential. In doing this, they often run counter to beliefs and practices which are of long-standing. The inevitable result is that the church begins to persecute them. Often, this persecution is calculating and ruthless. The young man is given a "label" which has taken on unsavory connotations in the minds of some, such as "radical," "fanatic," "liberal," or "heretic." The word is passed orally from person to person or from church to church, or in writing in personal letters or church publications of varying coverage. It is not long until no "sound" church will invite the young man to teach or preach. Like Jeremiah, he is "debarred from going to the house of the Lord" (36:5).

The young man may react in different ways, depending on the circumstances. Usually, he is forced to quit preaching in order to give his family some security for the future. (Like Paul, Jeremiah was not faced with this particular problem, 16:2). He learns quickly that it is useless to reason from the scriptures, because the die has already been cast. Thus, he goes into some other line of work, and the church loses the services of a man who could have been a great asset and blessing to God's people. Tragically, when this happens, some rejoice because the church has been spared from another extremist, while others just cannot understand why the young man was so weak in faith as to leave the ministry. Jeremiah never actually left the ministry, but by the very nature of the situation his effectiveness steadily decreased.

REVIEW QUESTIONS

1. Do you know of cases in which a capable, sincere young man entered the ministry only to be persecuted by the church because he tried to deal with the basic human problems and weaknesses which they displayed? React to this problem.

2. In your opinion, what kind of preaching does the church need most of all? Is it abstract, irrelevant messages, or is it practical, down-to-earth messages?

3. Name six ways suggested in this lesson in which God's people sometimes persecute preachers and teachers.

4. Do you know of cases in which church members tried to destroy a man's reputation by giving him a "label," or by slandering him or making accusations against him? How do you feel about this situation?

5. Do you know of preachers or teachers who have been imprisoned or killed because of their message? Discuss this.

6. Discuss the ways in which Jeremiah reacted to persecutions against him. Has any man ever reacted perfectly to persecution? Discuss this.

7. Discuss the problem of the church losing its young people, including young men who are preparing to preach and teach God's word. What do you feel can be done about this problem? Give specific personal examples if you know of some.

8. Discuss the possibility that the young man might actually be teaching non-biblical doctrines. What is the fair and right way to handle a problem of differences over teachings?

Lesson X

TWO EXAMPLES OF COMPLAINING - JEREMIAH AND HABAKKUK

"I will speak in the anguish of my spirit;
I will complain in the bitterness of my soul" (Job 7:11).

Jeremiah's Complaints

The book of Jeremiah contains five passages in which Jeremiah bitterly complains to God. An analysis of the matters which caused these complaints is very instructive.

1. The first passage is 11:18-12:6. Here Jeremiah complains about a personal problem and a spiritual problem. The personal problem was that he had loved and respected his family (see 12:6) and friends at his home town in Anathoth, but all the while they were plotting against him to kill him, saying:

> "Let us destroy the tree with its fruit,
> Let us cut him off from the land of the living,
> That his name be remembered no more" (11:19).

When Jeremiah learned about this plot, he prayed that God would take vengeance on these schemers (11:20; 12:3-4). The spiritual problem grew out of this personal problem. Jeremiah asks a question which has troubled man throughout the ages:

> "Why does the way of the wicked prosper?
> Why do all who are treacherous thrive?" (12:1).

It is difficult to reconcile logically the righteous rule of God over men with the fact that wicked people prosper. But for the man of faith, this dilemma must not be allowed to move him to doubt that God knows what He is doing with His world. If man could be God (which, of course, he cannot be), he might understand this problem immediately. God rebuked Jeremiah for becoming so upset about his opponents from Anathoth, because they were weak opponents in comparison with what Jeremiah would have to face later in Jerusalem. So God says to Jeremiah:

> "If you have raced with men on foot (the men of Anathoth), and they have wearied you,
> How will you compete with horses (the men of Jerusalem)?
> And if in a safe land you fall down,
> How will you do in the jungle of the Jordan?" (12:5).

2. The second passage appears in 15:15-21. Here Jeremiah complains because he had accepted the responsibility for preaching God's word to sinners (v. 16), had borne reproach because of his personal commitment to God (v. 15), and had denied himself the fellowship of his contemporaries (v. 17—"I sat alone"), and yet God had done nothing to help him bear his burden. He asks God:

> "Wilt thou be to me like a deceitful brook,
> Like waters that fail?" (v. 18).

This figure is based on the fact that during the summer season in Palestine almost all the rivers and streams run dry, so that the traveller cannot depend on them to quench his thirst (see also *Job* 6:14-20). When Jeremiah finished this complaint, God rebuked him for sin, and invited him to repent and turn back to God, promising him that if he did he would be with him so that his enemies would not prevail against him (vss. 19-21; see 1:8,19).

3. In the third passage, 17:14-18, Jeremiah tells God that his enemies rebuke him because some of the things which God told Jeremiah to predict had not yet come to pass (v. 15). The prophet reminds God that it was not his idea to announce doom, but he did so only because God told him to do so (v. 16). So he urges God to stand by him against his

persecutors, and not let them prevail over him (vss. 14, 17-18).

4. In the fourth passage, 18:19-23, the prophet reminds God that he had prayed for those who persecuted him that God would not destroy them (v. 20). But they continued to plot against him, and even tried to kill him (v. 23), therefore he urges God to destroy them (v. 21), and not forgive their iniquity (v. 23).

5. Jeremiah's bitterest complaint occurs in 20:7-18. He accuses God of persuading him to proclaim his words even though he did not really enjoy this (vss. 7-8). He has even tried to stop preaching, but God would not let him. He says:

> "If I say, 'I will not mention him,
> Or speak any more in his name,'
> There is in my heart, as it were a burning fire
> Shut up in my bones,
> And I am weary with holding it in,
> And I cannot" (v. 9).

He is grieved because all his familiar friends sought to overthrow him (v. 10). He bemoans the fact that he was ever born, since in his manhood he has had to accept the responsibility of telling his own people and friends and family that they are doomed (vss. 14-18).

Habakkuk's Complaints

The prophet Habakkuk was a contemporary of Jeremiah. The book of Habakkuk apparently records events in the prophet's life which took place shortly before the Babylonians established themselves as the most powerful kingdom on earth in 609 B.C. (See Lesson I). The whole book of Habakkuk is built around two complaints of the prophet, both of which are spiritual in nature.

1. First, Habakkuk could not understand why God was allowing the people of Judah to sin so much without punishing them. He says:

> "Destruction and violence are before me;
> Strife and contention arise.
> So the law is slacked
> And justice never goes forth.
> For the wicked surround the righteous,
> So justice goes forth perverted" (1:3-4).

In essence, this complaint is parallel to Jeremiah's first complaint. God's reply to Habakkuk is that God is in control of human history, and that He will punish His sinful people in His own good time and in His own way. He says: "I am rousing the Chaldeans" (1:6), who will overrun Judah to punish the people for their sins (1:7-11).

2. This reply poses a deeper problem for Habakkuk. How can God cause a nation more wicked than Judah to punish this less wicked nation? He says to God:

> "Thou who art of purer eyes than to behold evil
> And canst not look on wrong,
> Why dost thou look on faithless men,
> And art silent when the wicked swallows up
> The man more righteous than he?" (1:13).

God tells Habakkuk that although this may look inconsistent to man, God's way is above man's way, and ultimately those who are faithful will be delivered. In a very famous passage, God says:

> "If it seem slow, wait for it;
> It will surely come, it will not delay.
> Behold, he whose soul is not upright in him shall fail,
> But the righteous shall live (survive) by his faith
>   (faithfulness)" (2:3-4).

The point is that after God has finished using the Babylonians to punish His sinful people, He will punish the Babylonians as well.

Upon being told this, Habakkuk delivers a series of five woes against the Babylonians. (1) He condemns them because they plunder mercilessly and are so violent (2:6-8). (2) He derides them for getting gain by hurting others, and declares that by doing this they forfeit their own life.(2:9-11—see

Matthew 16:24-26). (3) He denounces them for destroying those who are weaker and priding themselves on their own achievements (2:12-14). (4) He chastens them for venting their wrath on those who could not defend themselves (2:15-17). (5) He chides them for trusting in idols made by the hands of men instead of in the living God (2:18-20).

The book of Habakkuk closes with a prayer, in which the prophet praises the Lord for His works in behalf of His people in former generations (3:1-15), and resolves to wait patiently as God carries out His plan in history. He says:

> "I will quietly wait for the day of trouble
> To come upon people who invade us" (3:16).

The Value of Complaining

There are different kinds of complaining. Much complaining is self-centered, and therefore is sinful. But it is quite possible that complaining represents a struggle taking place deep within the heart of a child of God, who is desperately wrestling with some of the great problems of human life. To be sure, this sort of complaining may involve sinning, as when Jeremiah charges God with treating men unfairly, or bemoans the day of his birth, or says that God has rejected him in time of dire need.

And yet, often an individual must pass through this sort of complaining quest, in which he says what he really feels and expresses his doubts frankly, in order to move away from his shallow faith to a deeper faith, which ultimately better equips him to serve God on a broader level. This seems to be what happened to Jeremiah and Habakkuk.

REVIEW QUESTIONS

1. What did Jeremiah complain about in 11:18-12:6? Do you face similar problems? How did God answer the prophet? Discuss.

2. What did Jeremiah complain about in 15:15-21? Do you ever feel that God has let you down? Discuss.

3. What did Jeremiah complain about in 17:14-18? Discuss.

4. What did Jeremiah complain about in 18:19-23? What portions of this complaint are good, and what portions are bad?

5. What did Jeremiah complain about in 20:7-18? Do you have some of the same problems? Discuss.

6. What was Habakkuk's first complaint? How did God answer this?

7. What was Habakkuk's second complaint? How did God answer this?

8. Give Habakkuk's five woes against the invading Babylonians. Are there any practical lessons which may be drawn from these?

9. Discuss whether complaining may be helpful to the man of faith.

Lesson XI

THE NATURAL RESPONSE TO GOD'S LOVE

"For the love of Christ leaves us no choice, when once we have reached the conclusion that one man died for all and therefore all mankind has died. His purpose in dying for all was that men, while still in life, should cease to live for themselves, and should live for him who for their sake died and was raised to life" (II Corinthians 5:14-15—NEB).

God's Love for His People

Like Hosea and Isaiah before him, Jeremiah continually reminded God's people of all the things which God had done for them. He specifically emphasized the great acts of God in Israel's history, as when He led Israel out of Egypt (2:6; 16:14), guided them through the wilderness (2:2,6), made a covenant with them at Sinai (11:2-4), gave them the promised land of Canaan (11:7; 11:5), and in time established the Davidic dynasty (23:5-6; 33:14-17). The reason that he did this was to urge the people to respond to God's love for them by loving Him and doing His will (7:22-25).

Also like Hosea and Isaiah, Jeremiah used a number of illustrations to emphasize the intimate personal relationship which God felt toward His people, and to show how Israel had flaunted God's love and thus had broken this relationship. (a) At the Exodus, God had taken Israel for his wife. At first she had loved her husband (2:2), but later she became unfaithful to Him and went after other lovers (the Canaanite Baals) (3:2; 18:13); therefore, the Lord was forced to give His wife a divorce (3:1). The Lord says:

"Surely, as a faithless wife leaves her husband,
So have you been faithless to me, O house of Israel"
(3:20).

(b) The relationship between God and Israel was like that of a father to his son. At first the son was loyal to his father (3:4), but in time he became unfaithful (3:22), so that God had to disown him. (c) As a good husbandman, God had planted Israel as a choice vine (2:21; 11:16), but when harvest time came, this vine produced bad fruit, and so had to be cut down (2:21; 12:10). (d) God worked carefully with Israel as a potter works with his clay to make it into a useful vessel. But Israel refused to respond to the molding hand of the potter, so He re-formed it into a vessel of destruction (i.e., a vessel worthy to be destroyed) (18:1-11). (3) The Lord tried to lead Israel as a shepherd leads his flock, but they turned each one to his own way, so that the flock was destined for destruction (13:17,20; 23:1-2). (f) Because of her sin, Israel was like a sick person, but without God (the great physician) there was no hope for healing the patient (6:7; 14:19; 30:12-15). It is noteworthy that the New Testament adopts these same illustrations in order to describe the relationship between Christ and the church.

Judah's Unnatural Response to God's Love

One might suppose that God's love for Israel would lead God's people naturally to love Him in return and thus to serve him. But Judah behaved in precisely the opposite way. Jeremiah vividly shows this "unnatural response" to God's love by using several illustrations drawn from everyday life.

1. He describes a thirsty traveller desperately searching for water. As he comes to a crossroads, he learns that if he goes in one direction, he will come to a beautiful stream fed by a fountain, where there is ample water for all men, but if he goes in the opposite direction he will come to some old cisterns which have collapsed and thus can hold no water. A man would naturally choose the road to the stream filled with water, but God says concerning Judah:

"My people have committed two evils:
They have forsaken me,
The fountain of living waters,
And hewed out cisterns for themselves,
Broken cisterns,
That can hold no water" (2:13; see also 17:13).

2. The prophet paints a picture of a wedding ceremony. Everything is ready for the service. Is it conceivable that the bride could forget her wedding dress or her ornaments? Of course not! This would be unthinkable. It would be unnatural! Yet, God's people do the unnatural thing in turning away from the Lord who loves them. Jeremiah asks:

"Can a maiden forget her ornaments,
Or a bride her attire?
Yet my people have forgotten me
Days without number" (2:32).

3. Even inanimate nature accepts its role in God's masterful universe. The waters of the ocean do not burst out beyond the limits which God has set for them, and yet God's people (who can respond to His love with knowledge and purpose of their own free will) are not satisfied with their lot in life, and thus they rebel against God. So God declares,

"Hear this, O foolish and senseless people,
Who have eyes, but see not,
Who have ears, but hear not.
Do you not fear me? says the Lord;
Do you not tremble before me?
I placed the sand as the bound for the sea,
A perpetual barrier which it cannot pass;
Though the waves toss, they cannot prevail,
Though they roar, they cannot pass over it.
But this people has a stubborn and rebellious heart;
They have turned aside and gone away" (5:21-23).

4. Jeremiah calls attention to a man walking down a road. If he stumbles and falls down, he immediately gets up, brushes himself off, and goes on. If he discovers that he is lost or that he has taken the wrong turn, he immediately retraces his steps or finds out where he is and how he can get to his destination. He does not have to be asked or forced to do this, because this is the natural thing to do. And yet,

God's people fall and they make no attempt to get up again; they become lost and put forth no effort to find their way back to God. The Lord says:

> "When men fall, do they not rise again?
> If one turns away, does he not return?
> Why then has this people turned away
> In perpetual backsliding?" (8:4-5).

5. At a certain time each year, migratory birds fly south. At another time of year, they return north. This often requires a flight of several hundred miles. But these birds do not have to be begged or forced to do this. It is an integral part of their nature. And yet, God's people do not love God for what He has done for them. The prophet says:

> "Even the stork in the heavens knows her times;
> And the turtledove, swallow, and crane keep the time
> of their coming;
> But my people know not the ordinance of the Lord"
> (8:7).

6. As long as the temperature is below freezing, snow does not melt, but stays on the crags of the Lebanon mountains in Palestine. This is just the way God has made it in nature. And yet God's people do the unnatural thing in abandoning the God who chose them and protected them and gave them the land of Canaan. God declares:

> "Does the snow of Lebanon leave the crags of Sirion?
> Do the mountain waters run dry, the cold flowing
> streams?
> But my people have forgotten me" (18:14-15).

The children of Jonadab and the children of Israel.

In Israel, there lived a very conservative monastic-type group called the Rechabites, whose origin can be dated back to their founder, Jonadab, who lived in the days of Jehu, the king of North Israel (see *II Kings* 10:15-24). Jonadab had taught his followers not to drink wine or build houses or plant vineyards, but to live in tents, and they did so. Some time during the reign of Jehoiakim (see *Jeremiah* 35:1),

Jeremiah went to the Rechabites, carrying some wine with him, and he said to them, "Drink wine" (35:5). But the Rechabites said to Jeremiah, "We will drink no wine, *for Jonadab the son of Rechab, our father, commanded us,* 'You shall not drink wine, neither you nor your sons for ever' " (35:6). The point is that the Rechabites did not drink wine *just because* their father (founder), Jonadab, had commanded them not to do so. But in contrast to this, Jeremiah points out that the Israelites had not obeyed God's commandments. God says: "The command which Jonadab the son of Rechab gave to his sons, to drink no wine, has been kept; and they drink none to this day, *for they have obeyed their father's command.* I have spoken to you persistently, *but you have not listened to me"* (35:14). How ironical it is that God's people are often less devoted to God, who has done so much for them, than others are to less worthy fathers or leaders.

The most significant thing in religion is motivation. If one is motivated by a genuine love for God because of what God has done for him, his religion is on a firm footing. He will be richly blessed, and his spiritual growth is certain.

> "Blessed is the man who trusts in the Lord,
> Whose trust is the Lord.
> He is like a tree planted by water,
> That sends out its roots by the stream,
> And does not fear when heat comes,
> For its leaves remain green,
> And is not anxious in the year of drought,
> For it does not cease to bear fruit" (17:7-8; see *Psalm* 1:1-3).

REVIEW QUESTIONS

1. Name some of the great acts of God in Israel's history mentioned by Jeremiah. From your own knowledge, name some of the great acts of God in Christian history. What is your own attitude toward what God has done for you?

2. State the six illustrations which Jeremiah uses to describe the intimate personal relationship between God and His people. Where are the same illustrations found in the New Testament? (Use a concordance, if necessary).

3. Give the six illustrations which Jeremiah uses to show that Israel was behaving unnaturally in the way she was reacting to God's love.

4. Which of these illustrations convey the most significant meaning to you? Discuss.

5. How did Jeremiah use the illustration of the Rechabites in order to teach Israel a great lesson?

6. What is the basic element in true religion? Discuss the problem of emphasis in religion. Do you feel it should be placed on obeying specific commandments or on the attitude of the heart, or both? Place the two in proper perspective.

Lesson XII

A BRIGHT FUTURE FOR THE FAITHFUL

"Trust in the Lord, and do good;
So you will dwell in the land, and enjoy security" *(Psalm*
37:3).

As the previous lessons have brought out, Jeremiah spent much of his time condemning sinners and warning them of impending doom. However, he did not do this because he enjoyed announcing a calamity which was about to come on God's people. As a matter of fact, he would rather tell the people that their future was filled with hope and security (see 17:16; 20:8-9; 28:1-6). But it was necessary for God to punish His people first in order to save them ultimately. Jeremiah had a few converts. In order to encourage them, he delivered a number of hope oracles, which painted a beautiful picture of a bright future for the faithful. A large number of these oracles have been grouped together in *Jeremiah* 30-33, which provides the biblical text for this lesson. The theme which seems to pervade these chapters is "I will restore the fortunes of Israel and Judah" (see 30:3, 18; 31:23; 32:44; 33:7,11,26). By studying these chapters carefully, it is possible to learn specifically what Jeremiah meant by this promise.

The Exiles Will Return to the Promised Land

Jeremiah declares that some of the Israelites and the Judeans who had been carried into exile would return to their land (see 30:31, 10-11; 31:4-19; 32:37; 33:6) in seventy years (29:10-11). In order to show that he was absolutely certain of this, while he was in prison during the tenth year of Zedekiah's reign during the Babylonian siege of

Jerusalem (32:1-2), Jeremiah bought the field of Hanamel, his uncle, at Anathoth (32:6-14). Then he explained to Baruch, his disciple and secretary, what this signified: "For thus says the Lord of hosts, the God of Israel: Houses and fields and vineyards shall again be bought in this land" (32:15; see also vss. 37, 41, 42-44).

Israel and Judah Will Be United Under One Leader

Jeremiah announces that when Israel and Judah return from exile, eventually they will be united under one leader as they had been under David and Solomon, and will no longer be divided (see 30:3-9). Using a word-play or pun based on the name of king Zedekiah (which means "The Lord is righteousness"), God declares:

> "In those days and at that time I will cause a righteous Branch to spring forth for David; and he shall execute justice and righteousness in the land. In those days Judah will be saved and Jerusalem will dwell securely. And this is the name by which it will be called: 'The Lord is our righteousness'" (33:15-16—see also 30:9; 33:23-26).

Essentially, this same promise appears in 23:5-8. A comparison of these passages with *Zechariah* 3:8-9 and 6:12-13 indicates that this "righteous Branch," the descendant of David, was Zerubbabel, the grandson of king Jehoiachin (Jeconiah—see *I Chronicles* 3:17-19). This is particularly clear from *Zechariah* 6:12, where the Lord says: "Behold, the man whose name is the Branch: for he shall grow up in his place, and he shall build the temple of the Lord," because *Ezra* 5-6 state that the temple was rebuilt under the leadership of Zerubbabel and Joshua (see especially *Ezra* 5:1-2; 6:13-15).

Israel's and Judah's Captors and Oppressors Will Be Overthrown

In order for God's people to be set free from their captivity, the nations which carried them into exile would have to be overthrown. And Jeremiah announces that God would do this. In a very straightforward manner, God says:

"I am with you to save you, . . .
I will make a full end of all the nations
Among whom I scattered you,
But of you I will not make a full end" (30:11).
(See also 30:8, 16, 20).

God's People Will Grow Numerically

Jeremiah announces that Israel and Judah will be restored to health as a physician heals his patient who has been very sick. God says:

"I will restore health to you,
And your wounds I will heal, . . .
Because they have called you an outcast:
'It is Zion, for whom no one cares!' " (30:17).

In the land of Canaan, they will greatly increase under God's blessing. God continues:

"I will multiply them, and they shall not be few;
I will make them honored, and they shall not be small" (30:19).

The Intimate Personal Relationship Between God and His People Will Be Re-established

As has been pointed out in Lesson IV, Jeremiah preached that the Lord was punishing Judah because the sins of God's people had become long-lived and deep-rooted. Their wicked hearts had turned away from God to selfish interests. Thus, it is not surprising to find that in the oracles of hope in *Jeremiah* 30-33, the emphasis is on the fact that God's main purpose is to rekindle that love for him which characterized Judah at the first (see 2:2). Sin had separated between Judah and her God (see *Isaiah* 59:2), but now God promises:

"You shall be my people,
And I will be your God" (30:22; cf. 31:1).

But standing in sin before God, Judah's restoration is impossible. Thus God declares that He will have mercy on his people; he will cleanse them and forgive them of their sins. In one passage, He says:

> "My heart yearns for him (i.e., Ephraim, cf. 31:18),
> I will surely have mercy on him" (31:20).

In another passage He promises: *"I will cleanse them* from all the guilt of their sin against me, and *I will forgive* all the guilt of their sin and rebellion against me" (33:8). God's forgiveness of man is a central teaching in the Old Testament just as it is in the New.

Jeremiah calls this forgiveness of God and the change of heart which it will produce in the lives of the Jews a "new covenant." He says that although Judah forsook God like an unfaithful wife forsakes her husband (31:32) because her religion was merely external and formal, now she will honor God as her husband and serve him *from the heart.* "This is the covenant which I will make with the house of Israel after those days, says the Lord: I will put my law within them, and I will write it *upon their hearts;* and I will be their God, and they shall be my people. And no longer shall each man teach his neighbor and each his brother, saying, 'Know the Lord,' for they shall all know me, from the least of them to the greatest, says the Lord; for I will forgive their iniquity, and I will remember their sin no more" (31:33-34). "To know" the Lord here means to have an intimate personal relationship with him, as is the case also in the book of Hosea (cf. 2:19-20). In a similar passage, God says: "I will give them one heart and one way, that they may fear me for ever . . . I will make with them *an everlasting covenant,* that I will not turn away from doing good to them; and I will put the fear of me *in their hearts,* that they may not turn from me" (32:39-40).

In its original context, *Jeremiah* 31:31-34 refers to a change of heart in the lives of Jews in Old Testament times, which God brought about by carrying His people into Babylonian exile. But early Christians saw that this passage captured the essence of the message of Jesus which they preached. So the writer of Hebrews applies it to Christianity (*Hebrews* 8:8-12). In view of the way in which he normally uses the Old Testament, apparently he looks on the change of heart which God wrought in the Jews through the exile (*Jeremiah* 31:31-34) as a *type* of the Christian religion, which emphasizes the necessity of serving God from the heart (see *Romans* 6:17; *Matthew* 15:8; *Hebrews* 10:22; etc.). For a study of how the New Testament uses the Old, see Volume 2, Lessons VII and VIII.

REVIEW QUESTIONS

1. What is the theme of *Jeremiah* 30-33? Read the passages which show this.

2. What are the five things included in this theme, according to the suggestions given in this lesson?

3. What did Jeremiah do to show that he was convinced that after seventy years, Jewish exiles would return to Jerusalem? Discuss this.

4. What did Jeremiah call the leader who would rule over God's people after the exile ended? What symbolic name did he give him? Who was this leader? Prove your answer from the Bible.

5. What had separated Judah from God? How did God plan to overcome this? Does the Old Testament teach that God forgives man's sins?

6. What was the "new covenant" mentioned in *Jeremiah* 31:33-34 and 32:40 in its original context? How does *Hebrews* 8:8-12 reapply *Jeremiah* 31:31-34?

7. Pick out three or four basic teachings of the book of Jeremiah which you have learned in the earlier lessons in this booklet. Discuss the importance of these in everyday life.

Lesson XIII

ZEPHANIAH AND NAHUM - JEREMIAH'S CONTEMPORARIES

"The Lord, your God, is in your midst;
You shall fear evil no more" (Zephaniah 3:15).

God's Way with Judah –Zephaniah

It is difficult to date the work of the prophet Zephaniah with absolute certainty, although it may be dated approximately. 1:1 indicates that he preached during the reign of Josiah (640-609 B.C.—See Lesson I). Zephaniah announced the fall of Nineveh, for he says:

> "And he (i.e., God) will stretch out his hand against
> the north,
> And destroy Assyria;
> And will make *Nineveh* a desolation" (2:13).

Since Nineveh fell in 612 B.C., this passage must be dated shortly before that time. Zephaniah condemned idolatry (1:4-5), foreign customs (1:8-9), etc., things which were destroyed in Josiah's reform which began in 621 B.C. These scant pieces of evidence seem to warrant dating the ministry of Zephaniah about 628-622 B.C., the years just before Josiah's reform.

Like Jeremiah, Zephaniah announced that the Lord is about to punish Judah and Jerusalem because of their continual sins. He pictures God as a priest who is about to offer a sacrifice. Jerusalem is that sacrifice, and the guests whom the Lord has invited are enemy armies (in Zephaniah's historical situation, perhaps the Scythians). The prophet says:

> "The day of the Lord is at hand;
> The Lord has prepared a sacrifice
> And consecrated his guests" (1:7; see also 1:4, 14-16).

Zephaniah names several specific sins which explain why Judah's punishment was inevitable. These are sins which seem to characterize God's people to some degree in every generation. (a) Zephaniah rebukes the Jews because they are not wholly committed to God's service, but have a divided loyalty. God warns:

> "I will stretch out my hand against Judah, . . .
> (Against) those who bow down and swear to the Lord
> And yet swear by Milcom" (1:4-5).

Milcom was the god of the Ammonites (*I Kings* 11:5,33), and a few years (or possibly months) after Zephaniah issued this oracle, Josiah destroyed the idol of Milcom in Jerusalem (*II Kings* 23:13). (b) The prophet denounces the wicked leaders of God's people, who are not genuinely concerned about the well-being of the people under them, but only about their own gain. He says:

> "Her officials within her are roaring lions;
> Her judges are evening wolves that leave nothing till the morning.
> Her prophets are wanton, faithless men;
> Her priests profane what is sacred, they do violence to the law" (3:3-4).

(c) Zephaniah reproves God's people because they are so calloused that they feel no shame when they sin. He refers to them as a "shameless nation" (2:1), and declares that even though their God is righteous and does no wrong, His people know no shame (3:5). (d) The prophet condemns the people for their indifference. In announcing His punishment on His people, God says:

> "At that time I will search Jerusalem with lamps (see
> *Jeremiah* 5:1),
> And I will punish the men who are thickening upon
> their lees" (1:12).

Here, Zephaniah is comparing the men of Judah with wine, which must be constantly stirred and poured from vat to vat in order to prevent it from becoming too sweet and too thick, and thus lacking in proper strength and taste (see *Jeremiah* 48:11 for a vivid description of this process). The New Testament denounces indifference in the early church (see *Romans* 13:11-12; *Revelation* 3:14-22), and this has proved to be an erosive power in the church throughout the generations. (e) Zephaniah rebukes God's people because they trust in wealth, believing that it has the ability to rescue them from every calamity. The prophet says that riches will be worthless when God's punishment comes.

> "Neither their silver nor their gold
> Shall be able to deliver them
> On the day of the wrath of the Lord" (1:18).

(f) The prophet chides God's people because they have not responded to His correction by repenting and turning to Him. He says of Jerusalem:

> "She listens to no voice,
> She accepts no correction" (3:2).

And again God says:

> "I said, 'Surely she will fear me,
> She will accept correction; . . .
> But all the more they were eager
> To make all their deeds corrupt" (3:7).

(g) Behind all of these sins lay pride. Perhaps it would not be incorrect to suggest that pride is a prime motivation for the large majority of human sins. God announces:

> "I will remove from your midst
> Your proudly exultant ones,
> And you shall no longer be haughty
> In my holy mountain" (3:11).

But (again like Jeremiah) Zephaniah did not preach that God's purpose ultimately was to destroy His people, but rather that He was punishing them to bring them to repentance and salvation. He promises that the Lord will "restore their fortunes" (2:7). God's chastising will humble some of his people and they will seek refuge in Him (3:12). Apparently, it is with this "remnant" in mind (see 2:9) that Zephaniah joyfully proclaims:

> "The Lord has taken away the judgments against you,
> He has cast out your enemies.
> The King of Israel, the Lord, is in your midst;
> You shall fear evil no more" (3:15).

God's Way With a Foreign Nation—Nahum

The entire book of Nahum consists of oracles announcing the fall of Nineveh, the capital of Assyria (see in particular 2:8; 3:7,18, where Nineveh or Assyria is specifically mentioned). Thus, it is generally agreed that the ministry of Nahum reflected in this little prophetic book comes from about 614 B.C., i.e., a couple of years before this city fell. It is interesting to note that the prophet states that Nineveh is no better than Thebes (or No-Amon), the capital of southern Egypt, which was overthrown by the Assyrian king Ashurbanipal in 663 B.C. (3:8-10).

Nahum describes in great detail how enemy armies will come down upon Nineveh, burst through its walls, and raze the city to the ground. In a most graphic poem, he says:

> "Woe to the bloody city,
> All full of lies and booty—
> No end to the plunder!
> The crack of whip, and rumble of wheel,
> Galloping horse and bounding chariot!
> Horsemen charging,
> Flashing sword and glittering spear,
> Hosts of slain,
> Heaps of corpses,
> Dead bodies without end—
> They stumble over the bodies" (3:1-3).

According to Nahum, the reason Nineveh fell is because God was punishing her for her continual sins (the same reason that God punished Jerusalem!). The prophet specifically mentions three sins which characterized Nineveh. (a) The people of Nineveh worshipped idols rather than the one true God, so God declares:

> "From the house of your gods I will cut off
> The graven image and the molten image" (1:14).

(b) The Assyrian armies had ruthlessly overrun and destroyed other nations. Nahum compares their attacks with that of a lion pouncing on his prey.

> "The lion tore enough for his whelps
> And strangled prey for his lionesses;
> He filled his caves with prey
> And his dens with torn flesh" (2:12).

(c) Nineveh was filled with pride. She boasted of her own strength, her large numbers of able-bodied men, and her wealth (see 1:12; 2:9; 3:15-17). But the Lord declares:

> "Though they be strong and many,
> They will be cut off and pass away" (1:12).

God's Way in His World

When God sent Jonah to preach Nineveh's overthrow, His real intention was to try to bring Nineveh to repentance. When Jeremiah and Zephaniah declared that Jerusalem would be overthrown, their purpose was to try to bring God's people to repentance. Therefore, it seems logical to believe that when Nahum announced the overthrow of Nineveh, his ultimate hope that was Nineveh might somehow be brought to repentance. As with Jonah and the oracles concerning foreign nations in *Isaiah* 13-23; *Jeremiah* 46-51; *Ezekiel* 25-32; and *Amos* 1-2, the basic assumption of the book of Nahum seems to be that God is gravely concerned not only with His chosen people, but also with all mankind, in Old Testament times as well as in New Testament times.

For one who takes biblical teaching seriously, the belief

that God works in the affairs of men in every age is central. Although the man of faith may not fully comprehend how God works or what He is trying to accomplish, he accepts the biblical interpretation which affirms that God works through His people for the ultimate salvation of all men.

REVIEW QUESTIONS

1. Give the possible dates for Zephaniah's prophetic ministry. State the arguments which support your position (It does not have to agree with the position taken in this lesson).

2. What figure did Zephaniah use to announce that God was about to punish Judah and Jerusalem?

3. List the seven sins which Zephaniah singles out as causes for the downfall of Jerusalem. Discuss each of these in light of the relevance which they might have for man's sins in the modern world.

4. Who or what was Milcom? Prove your answer from the Bible.

5. What figure did Zephaniah use to condemn Judah for her indifference? Discuss this figure, and the problem of indifference in the modern church.

6. Was Zephaniah a "prophet of doom" only, or did he see a bright future for some of God's people? Discuss.

7. What was the subject of Nahum's preaching? With the fall of what city did he compare the fall of Nineveh?

8. According to Nahum, what sins led to Nineveh's downfall?

9. Do you believe that God was concerned about all nations in Old Testament times? Justify your answer from the Bible. Do you believe that God works among nations in the modern world? Discuss.

BIBLIOGRAPHY

These three Volumes on the Old Testament Prophets have been designed for the person just beginning a serious study of prophetic literature. It has been thought best to avoid all references to other works except when absolutely necessary. The primary emphasis is on theology or religious teaching in the prophetic books, although attention has been given to some critical matters, especially in Volume I.

The literature on the Old Testament Prophets is immense in the English language, to say nothing of studies in German, French, Dutch, Italian, and the Scandinavian languages. A person could devote himself to studies in the prophets for the rest of his life, and still not be able to read all which has been written. Thus, the present writer offers the following bibliography as a tiny sampling of helpful works, in hopes that the student who is genuinely interested in an in-depth study of the Prophets will realize that he must go far, far beyond what is suggested here.

Introductions to Prophetic Literature and Theology

Lindblom, Johannes. *Prophecy in Ancient Israel.* Oxford: Basil Blackwell, 1962.
von Rad, Gerhard. *Old Testament Theology.* Volume II. Trans. D.M.G. Stalker. London: Oliver and Boyd, 1967.
Scott, R.B.Y. *The Relevance of the Prophets.* Revised edition. New York: The Macmillan Company, 1968. (Paperback).
Smith, George Adam. *The Book of the Twelve Prophets.* Two Volumes. London: Hodder and Stoughton, 1896.

Commentary Sets

The Anchor Bible. Garden City, New York: Doubleday & Company, 1965ff.
The Interpreter's Bible. Nashville: Abingdon Press, 1956.
The International Critical Commentary. New York: Charles Scribner's Sons, 1905-1912.

> *The Old Testament Library.* Philadelphia: The Westminster Press, 1969ff.
> *Torch Bible Commentaries.* London: SCM Press, Ltd., 1962ff.

One Volume Commentaries

> *The Interpreter's One-Volume Commentary on the Bible.* Nashville: Abingdon Press, 1971.
> *The Jerome Biblical Commentary.* Englewood Cliffs, N.J.: Prentice-Hall, Inc., 1968.
> *Peake's Commentary on the Bible.* London: Thomas Nelson and Sons Ltd., Reprinted 1967.

Special Studies on Particular Aspects of Prophetic Material

> Hammershaimb, E. *Some Aspects of Old Testament Prophecy from Isaiah to Malachi.* Kobenhavn: Rosenkilde og Bagger, 1966.
> Lewis, Jack P. *Minor Prophets.* Austin, Texas: R. B. Sweet Co., Inc., 1966.
> Rowley, H. H., editor. *Studies in Old Testament Prophecy presented to T. H. Robinson.* Edinburgh: T&T Clark, 1946. Reprinted 1957.
> Rowley, H. H. *The Servant of the Lord and Other Essays on the Old Testament.* Oxford: Basil Blackwell, 1965.
> Westermann, Claus. *Basic Forms of Prophetic Speech.* Trans. H. C. White. Philadelphia: The Westminster Press, 1967.

Journals dealing with Prophetic Literature quite extensively

Biblica
Catholic Biblical Quarterly
The Expository Times
Harvard Theological Review
Hebrew Union College Annual
Interpretation
Journal of Biblical Literature
Journal of Theological Studies
Restoration Quarterly
Vetus Testamentum
Zeitschrift für die alttestamentliche Wissenschaft